25 GOLDEN YEARS OF
CLASSIC
American Cars
1945-1970

25 GOLDEN YEARS OF

CLASSIC

American Cars

1945-1970

CLB

Acknowledgements

The publishers would like to offer their special thanks to the following for their
invaluable assistance in the preparation of this book:
Auburn-Cord-Duesenberg Museum, Auburn, Indiana.
Curt Marketti
Skip and Cathy Marketti
Sanderson's Auto Sales, Auburn, Ind.
Gary and Lori Shuman
The Randinelli family
Don Peterson
Charles Coleman and 'Toni'
Ben Caskey and family
Rick Carroll
The Elliott Museum, Jensen Beach, Fla.
Tom Lester
The Riekes
Hadzera Wright
All photographs shot using an Asahi Pentax 6x7 camera with 150mm Takumar
lens. Processing by Langley Colour, Langley St., London WCl
Unique Color Lab., Cass St., Fort Wayne, Indiana.
Sources: Motor Trend, Consumer Guide Cars of the 50s, Cars of the Sixties, Car
Life, Car Exchange, Special Interest Autos, Floyd Clymer's 1950 to 1955 Catalog of
Automobiles series, Crestline's Chevrolet, Chrysler and Buick books.

Featuring the Photography of Nicky Wright
0930 Classic American Cars
This edition published in 1997 by CLB
Distributed in the USA by BHB International Inc.,
30 Edison Drive, Wayne, New Jersey 07470
© 1992 CLB International, Godalming, Surrey, England
All rights reserved
Printed in Hong Kong
ISBN 1-85833-749-6

Dep. Leg. B. 21.189/83

It was Sunday, September 2nd 1945 and on board U.S. battleship *Missouri* berthed in Tokyo Bay, General Douglas MacArthur, as Supreme Commander of the Allied Powers, conducted the brief, but formal ceremony of Japan's surrender. The guns fell silent and the sun, as if on cue, broke through the clouds. Three years, eight months and 25 days after Pearl Harbor, the curtain finally closed on World War Two. Now the victorious warriors could return home to loved ones, to interrupted careers…and a new car.

Or so Detroit, America's automotive capital, hoped. Not that the car makers worried, for three and three quarter years is a long time to go without the chance to buy a new car. All through the conflict, auto factories had been kept busy supplying the Allies with weapons of war although a few 1942 models, kept in storage on government orders, managed to sneak out to high priority customers. But from July 1945 onward, in anticipation that war's end was in sight, the auto companies began to convert their factories back to civilian use in readiness for the car buying boom.

Not many cars left the factories during the closing months of 1945 and those that did were classed as 1946 models. To call them 1946 models was a bit of an anachronism because they were really 1942 cars warmed over with a few changes of trim here and there. This was due, in part, to material shortages following the war, but Chrysler at least made a few token changes to the old styling, enabling it to call its products "new" with a reasonably clear conscience.

Chrysler also ushered in an entirely new model…well, almost. This was the Town & Country two-door convertible and four-door sedan. The name Town and Country was not new and had been used on Chrysler division's first station wagon, the Royal Town & Country, in 1941. Designed by David A. Wallace, Chrysler Divison's president, the wagon was notable for its white ash framing and mahogany veneer panelling. The 1946 version continued its forebear's use of ash frames and mahogany panels, setting it apart from its contemporaries. In fact, Wallace's concept was extremely attractive and in its eight-cylinder, convertible form was the industry's first production "personal car," some two decades before Ford described its Thunderbird as such.

The showrooms were filled to overflowing; no matter the cars were reincarnated '42s; the public were in no mood to care. They wanted anything that had new paint and shiny chrome and the manufacturers were hard-put to keep up with demand. Ford and Chevrolet churned out the most, with 372,917 and 397,104 units respectively, while the smaller independent companies, though not in the same league, posted very healthy sales returns. And what of Plymouth, traditionally occupying third place behind Ford and Chevy? Unit production in 1946 was 242,534, more than enough to help keep Chrysler Corporation in second place overall, a position the company had snatched from Ford back in 1936.

There were newcomers, too. Quite a few people foresaw the post-war automobile boom and determined to get in on the act. Throughout the late 'forties, all manner of strange, wheeled contraptions came tumbling out of garden sheds and the like. Most survived little more than a year or two before dashing themselves to pieces on the broken backs of their creators' heady dreams. Some, like the Bobbi-Kar mini, showed promise; it had independent four-wheel suspension, plastic body and various air- or water-cooled rear engines of diminutive size. Lack of money hastened its early demise but it bounced back in modified form as the Keller. After two years, and 18 pilot models, the Keller, too, went into limbo.

If the ground was littered with failed attempts there were a few, very few, who managed to break through the ordered ranks of automotive commerce and make a success of things, even if only for a short time. The Kaiser-Frazer Corporation was an excellent case in point.

Although Joseph Washington Frazer came from an aristocratic background he eschewed high society life to concentrate on a career with his first love, the motor industry. In the 'twenties and 'thirties he made quite a name for himself, assisting Walter P. Chrysler in his early days – it was he who christened Chrysler's low-priced model, the Plymouth – injected new lifeblood into Willys-Overland and took over the collapsed Graham-Paige Company with the idea of producing a new car after his name.

To build a car would require considerable finance, and to this end Frazer discussed his ideas with Henry J. Kaiser, a man who had made a fortune out of gravel and Liberty ships. The result of these discussions was the Kaiser-Frazer Corporation, launched in July 1945.

The fledgling company purchased an enormous factory once used for building bombers, at Willow Run, Michigan. Two models were to be produced: a low medium-priced car called the Kaiser and the more expensive Frazer. Initial plans called for a radical departure from the conventional norm; front-wheel drive, four-wheel independent suspension and unitary construction graced K-85, the Kaiser

prototype. For one reason or another, fully explained in Richard Langworth's excellent book, "The Last Onslaught on Detroit", when Kaiser and Frazer started production in June 1946 they were entirely conventional apart from their slab-sided styling.

Kaiser-Frazer built 11,753 cars in 1946, 144,507 the following year, a staggering number for a new company, and a total that took K-F to eighth place overall in the sales charts, ahead of established makes like Mercury and Studebaker. New styling had a lot to do with K-F's success but the motoring pundits hedged their bets, preferring to wait and see how the newcomer would fare against the established manufacturers' newly designed post-war models waiting in the wings.

Passenger car production for 1946 ended with 2,155,171 units flooding the sellers' market – the best the industry had seen in years. Everybody had money in their jeans and a new set of wheels was top of their wants list. Detroit responded with more of the same for 1947 apart from Studebaker, who, alone among the established companies, had introduced brand-new styling the previous spring. The car's shape was initiated at the Loewy Studios under the direction of Virgil M. Exner, the man responsible for Chrysler styling from 1954-1962.

Exner had a difference of opinion with Raymond Loewy and left, setting up his own studio outside South Bend, Studebaker's home base. He continued to work on the 1947 design and the result was an amalgam of Loewy and Exner ideas. The finished car was distinguished by its short hood and smooth profile which flowed into the swept-back rear fender bulge. From the rear, the Studebaker looked not unlike the front of an airliner cockpit, its U-shaped rear window, supported by three slender pillars, curving almost to the door edge of the coupe model.

What of the power plants those first few years after the war? Cadillac stayed with its venerable L-head V-8 until 1949, Buick remained faithful to the OHV straight eight until 1953, while Ford's 100hp L-head V-8 continued to blow rival Chevrolet and Plymouth L-head sixes into the weeds. New boy K-F used a modified version of the Continental "Red Seal" industrial in-line six and Lincoln was the sole survivor of the great multi-cylinder period before the war, its 292 cubic-inch L-head V-12 producing 125hp.

America entered 1948 with President Truman elected to serve a further four-year term. Unlike Europe, still suffering the after-effects of war, America and Americans were enjoying the good life. Steel was in plentiful supply and the motor industry was in full swing capitalising on the unprecedented sales boom. Although a complete change-over to new designs was still a year away, Cadillac, Packard and Hudson introduced theirs as 1948 models.

Car stylists had a field day during those halcyon years, for nobody was sure how the buying public would react to any given style. Given an almost free hand, the stylists were able to design what they thought would capture the imagination. Therefore, the public had a number of highly individual cars to choose from; uniformity would only come once a "styling leader" had been established.

Harley Earl, GM's brilliant head of styling, was the progenitor of the tail-fin, Cadillac's styling coup for 1948. He and members of his team from GM's Art & Color Design Studio, had been inspired by the shape of the P.38 Lightning fighter, a beautiful design in its own right, and paid homage to the aircraft with subtle references to its overall concept which were employed in the new Cadillac. The standout features, of course, were the tailfins, and outrageous as they may seem they actually enhanced an already attractive design. From 1948 until the mid-sixties, the tailfin became a Cadillac trademark.

In another part of Detroit, Hudson was readying its sleek new line. Designed by in-house stylists led by Frank Spring, the new Hudsons boasted clean, aerodynamic lines devoid of unnecessary gimmicks. Due to its extremely low roofline, the Hudson featured a lowered floor known as the Step-Down design – ergo, you didn't step in; you stepped down.

Hudsons came with a unitary body and chassis, a characteristic of the marque since 1932, and a new 262 cubic-inch Super Six engine developing 121hp. An L-head design, the engine proved extremely durable and was a hot performer. With a new engine and design, 1948 was Hudson's best year with production totalling 143,697 units and profits of over $13 million.

Packard had made a name for itself as purveyors of fine motor cars for almost half a century; they were to Americans what Rolls-Royce is to the British. In 1948 Packard unveiled its new models which were a complete departure from the classic, traditional shapes long associated with the company's name. Gone was the elegant grille, flowing fenders – hallmarks of Howard Darrin's classic 1941 styling – which were replaced by a slab-sided design many people unkindly likened to a pregnant elephant.

Packard used the old body fitted with new side panels to obtain the flow-through fender look. A bulbous, flatter hood and squat grille finished the transformation and although traditional quality remained – well, it just didn't look like a Packard. Still, it sold extremely well in both six and eight cylinder forms. Production ran to 92,000 cars in 1948 and a further 115,000 in 1949, Packard's best sales year since the company began.

1948 finished with almost four million automobiles produced; even the diminutive four-cylinder Crosley did well. Nearly 25,000 Crosleys were built but it was to be the last time the little company saw five-figure production totals. At least they survived a further four years which is more than can be said for one struggling, forward looking concern. The story of Preston Tucker and his dream to produce an automobile 30 years ahead of its time reads rather like a Shakespearean tragedy.

Born in Michigan in 1903, Tucker became interested in automobiles at an early age. He held a variety of jobs and was a policeman for a time but selling cars was something he could do very successfully. He was also something of an inventor and designed a swivelling gun turret which was bought by the army. With money in hand Tucker saw the way clear to fulfil his dream... to build his own car.

After the war he rented a disused, Chicago based B-29 bomber factory from the War Assets Administration. Then he hired stylists Alex Tremulis and Philip Egan – the latter of G. Lippincott & Co. of New York – to design a truly advanced car. He wanted four-wheel disc brakes, all independent suspension, rear-mounted engine and a host of safety features built in. Unfortunately money was running out so Tucker sold shares in his company enthusiastically promising full-scale production within a few months.

Enthusiasm doesn't pay bills, his promises didn't hold water and soon the Securities and Exchange Commission were investigating his affairs. They found a few irregularities but after a lengthy hearing allowed him to continue to try and raise capital through stock, provided he met certain conditions.

Tucker was a brilliant salesman and made use of his talents in a huge publicity campaign. Full-page advertisements appeared in newspapers and magazines, photographs were issued showing workers in a busy factory. But still no cars, just more promises. Money kept drying up and some of his directors resigned. He was hounded by the SEC and a senator demanded an investigation. Rashly, Tucker said he would be producing 1000 cars a week by March 1948. This, of course, didn't happen; instead 50 were put together by hand.

Several Tuckers were taken to Indianapolis Speedway for testing and there was no doubt these examples were bona fide, and what is more, excellent cars. Perhaps everything would work out in Tucker's favour, after all.

Drew Pearson, a well known newspaper columnist, went on radio and branded Tucker and his organisation as a sham. He alleged he had proof it was all a con. Tucker sent a furious letter to the U.S. Dept. of Justice accusing Pearson and the established car-makers of trying to crush him. But it was too late. Shortly after, the SEC arraigned Tucker on charges of fraud.

The hearings and court case took an eternity but Tucker was finally cleared of all charges brought against him. By now the damage was done. There was no money left and the world had moved on. Right up to his death in 1956, Tucker was still trying to raise interest in his car. That he was still trying shows the man wasn't a crook... a real con-man wouldn't try the same dodge twice if he'd been found out the first time. Tucker's only crime was his own optimism coupled with a large dose of naïvety. Whatever anybody's opinion, there can be no denying the excellence of his 50 cars... all but one survive to this day.

As the Tucker died, so too did America's last 12-cylinder engine. Lincoln had continued using its L-head V-12 in its post-war models from 1946 to 1948 but sales, especially in 1948, had been disappointing. Not that it was an unattractive car; Lincoln and its higher priced sister, the Continental, had stuck to 1942 styling along with everyone else and apart from the jazzier, post-war grille they were handsome cars, the convertible arguably the best looking of all.

New models were in the works for 1949 and Lincoln's policy was to concentrate on high volume cars rather than continue with necessarily low production, expensive cars like the Continental. The V-12 engine, long in the tooth and with a history of unreliability due to ring wear and inadequate water passages among other things, was discarded in favour of a 337 c.i.d. L-head V-8. The end of the V-12 was the end of an era of graceful, powerful multi-cylinder cars that reached a peak during the 'thirties.

The new Lincolns ushered in new models from all Ford divisions for 1949. Ford introduced its totally new line in June of 1948 and they were, in terms of styling, a complete departure from the past. They were also, in many people's opinion, the most attractive of the low-priced three; Chevrolet and Plymouth

had new designs for 1949 but Ford's break with tradition was more complete. A youthful Henry Ford II had taken over at the helm of the mighty company his grandfather had built, on September 21st, 1945. He had done so only on the understanding he would have a free hand to make whatever changes he deemed necessary, and old Henry, not always the easiest of men to deal with, had grudgingly concurred.

The first results of Henry Ford II's reign manifested itself in a new 1946 model crafted from the old. This was the Ford Sportsman convertible and what made it different from the rest of the model line was its wood panelling with mahogany inserts grafted onto the body structure. The idea had come from E. T. Gregorie, the brilliant designer, cultivated by the equally brilliant and forward looking Edsel Ford, whose untimely death in 1943 robbed the motoring world of one of its great talents. It also robbed Ford of Gregorie who left the company in 1946.

The Sportsman and its lookalike cousin, the longer wheelbase Mercury Sportsman, although attractive, were largely ignored by the public perhaps because Chrysler's Town & Country had cornered the market with an admittedly more luxurious and "newer" looking car. Only 3,692 Ford and Mercury Sportsman models were built before it was dropped in 1948.

The 1949 Fords and sister divisions, Mercury and Lincoln, represented the greatest change in FoMoCo products since the Model A. Gone were the archaic beam front axle and transverse leaf suspension to be replaced by coil sprung independent front suspension and the live rear axle was located by longitudinal leaf springs. The cars had new transmissions, hypoid final drive did away with the old spiral-bevel arrangement and overdrive was an option.

A new OHV V-8 would not arrive until 1954 so Ford stuck to its tried and true L-head design; the hot rod fraternity's darling. The old engine pumped out 100hp in stock trim and was capable of holding its own against anything the opposition offered.

Sharing its basic shell with the new Lincoln, the 1949 Mercury was styled by E. T. Gregorie. It had started out as the new Ford but had been upgraded to Mercury. The Ford was the work of freelance stylist Richard Caleal, under the guidance of company design consultant George Walker. Looking at the two cars side by side the different design philosophy becomes readily apparent; Caleal's Ford has smooth, albeit slab-sided styling whereas the Mercury's shape is more bulbous, with a high waistline, narrow glass area, low roof and stepped fenders. On the mechanical side Mercury was almost identical to Ford but the engine was tweaked to give 110 hp.

As far as today's collectors are concerned, the 1949-1951 Mercurys are the cream of Ford's early post-war crop. They became a favourite with 'fifties customisers and James Dean drove one in "Rebel Without a Cause". Nostalgia movies such as "Graffitti" and "Last Picture Show" also featured Mercurys as symbols of 'fifties youth.

When Henry Ford II took over the company was dying on its feet and losing some $10 million a month. Ever since Chrysler grabbed second place in 1936, Ford fortunes had been on the wane, partly due to the elder Henry's reluctance to move with the times. Working closely with a team of new, forward looking planners, Henry Ford II turned the company around and it recorded a $177 million profit – its first for many a year – for 1949. Even more satisfying for Ford was the recapture of the Number Two position from Chrysler.

Kaufman Thuma Keller became head of Chrysler in 1935. What he inherited from its founder Walter P., was a healthy organisation whose success was attributed to well engineered cars. After the war, company policy under Keller was engineering first and foremost. The cars were designed the way the engineers wanted instead of as practised by their rivals at Ford and GM. This was all very laudable but not necessarily saleable. The post-war climate, set fair for styling, was probably encouraged by GM, whose Art & Color Design Studio perceived the mood and prepared the way. Compare GM's graceful and clearcut 1949 designs with Chrysler's upright, square and boxy proportions not forgetting Ford's sleek, brilliantined good looks and it is easy to see why Chrysler tumbled.

Not that Chrysler fell that much... that was to come a little later. Although uninspired, the company still had enough loyal followers who deemed practicality better than pizzazz. 1,033,000 assorted Chryslers, Dodges, DeSotos and Plymouths found their way into welcoming ownership, more in 1950. But here's the rub: Chevrolet's 1949 models accounted for 1,109,000 of GM's total sales while the fleet Buick produced almost 400,000 units. Talking of which, the '49 Buick Roadmaster in its two-door fastback version, was one of the prettiest cars to emerge during the year. A toothy, heavily chromed grille, later to be dubbed "The Million Dollar Grin", set off its rounded, aircraft fuselage theme. Unlike Ford,

Hudson and others, Buick, along with all of GM's lines, retained a rear fender outline emphasised by a chrome splash-guard in front of the skirted wheel opening. A distinctive styling touch were the "portholes" at the rear of each front fender. These became a Buick trademark and have remained, in one form or another, ever since.

Mechanically, Buicks were much the same as earlier models. The OHV Fireball Straight Eight continued in 248 and 320 cubic inch versions but a runaway success was the optional Dynaflow automatic transmission, offered initially on the top-of-the-line Roadmaster series, when it was introduced in 1948. Its popularity even surprised Buick, who doubled production to meet the demand, making it also available in the Super series.

Cadillac had restyled in 1948 and remained much the same for '49 with one important exception. It threw a brand-new OHV V-8 into the arena, sharing the accolades with sister division Oldsmobile, which had designed its own OHV V-8 independently of Cadillac. Both engines were short-stroke high compression units designed for the better postwar fuels. Of the two, Cadillac's was the larger, displacing 331 c.i.d. versus 303 for the Olds. Developing 160hp at 3,800 rpm, Cadillac's engine was 200 pounds lighter than the old L-head it replaced, could reach 100 mph and accomplish 0-60 in around 13 seconds.

Oldsmobile's design had an oversquare configuration (bore and stroke was 3.75 × 3.44 inches) and developed 135hp at 3600 rpm. In stock form it had a compression ratio of 7.25:1 but was designed to go up to 12:1 should ever the need arise. Originally intended only for the luxurious 98 Series, Oldsmobile heads decided it would suit the lesser 88 Series as well. Known as the Rocket 88, the smaller Oldsmobile became a must for NASCAR drivers who drove them to Championship points time after time for two years. On the other hand, big sister Cadillac went racing at Le Mans. Wealthy sportsman Briggs Cunningham was so struck with the new engine that he took two Cadillacs – one a stock Series 62 sedan, the other a Cunningham design affectionately dubbed "Le Monstre" by the French – and raced them in the 24-hour classic. At the end of the race the stock Cadillac came in tenth, just ahead of "Le Monstre". The results were amazing for a new engine not designed for racing and proved what a durable and versatile power plant it was. The result must have pleased designers Ed N. Cole, Harry F. Barr and John F. Gordon, who had spent ten years developing it.

The year ended with overall industry production of over five million units making it the best year ever. All, except the little Crosley, increased their sales and Nash's new aerodynamic, Airflyte 600 and more expensive Ambassador models catapulted the independent into tenth place, past Hudson and Chrysler. Production totals soared again for 1950, in spite of the June 12th invasion of South Korea by the Communist North. Once again, the Allies had a war on their hands, this one euphemistically described as a "policing action". Early successes by General MacArthur's forces pointed to an end by Christmas.

Apart from 6½ million units produced for the year, most manufacturers stood pat after all-new cars in 1949. Changes, if any, were mainly cosmetic; Buick's grille looked like somebody with buck teeth and was rather ugly compared to the previous year. Chevrolet became the first of the low-priced cars to offer an automatic transmission. Christened Powerglide, it had two forward speeds, reverse and was of the torque converter type. Automatics were making great strides; Cadillac, Olds and Pontiac shared Hydramatic, Buick had its Dynaflow and Chrysler divisions had a semi-automatic called Fluid-Drive, but Ford was still working on its own unit. Lincoln, however, offered GM's Hydramatic as an option. Packard was the only independent to design and produce its own automatic transmission, the Ultramatic, which was quite similar to Buick's Dynaflow. Studebaker's automatic was designed in conjunction with Borg-Warner.

Besides the rapid development of automatics, other convenience items began to appear with more regularity. Power windows, convertible tops, steering, brakes and even air conditioning were there for the asking. By the end of the decade, 90% of American cars would be equipped with automatics while power steering and brakes would command as high a percentage. In the case of luxury cars many of these items would be standard fare.

The 'fifties decade can best be described as a period of over abundance in almost everything you can think of. As far as the motor industry was concerned it is perhaps more accurate to qualify it as having reached boiling point and not knowing when to turn down the heat. It was an era of longer, lower, wider, furious competition, the horsepower race and the deaths of several household names not strong enough to sustain the pace.

One of the first to die was Crosley. A mini-compact from the day it was launched in 1939, Crosley, though austere in design, was quite radical in concept. It started its life with a little 35.3 cubic inch air-cooled four-cylinder engine developing 12hp. During the war, Crosley built an overhead cam four-cylinder engine for the U.S. Navy and used a block made from brazed copper and sheet steel. This engine was used in Crosley's post-war cars up to 1949 but, due to electrolysis, a difficulty associated with copper/steel mixes under various conditions, holes would appear in the cylinders. The expense of fitting new engines prompted Crosley to switch to a cast-iron block, thereby curing the problem.

Crosley sales were pretty good up to 1949 but new models from the stronger independents and the Big Three produced a dramatic down-turn in the company's fortunes. Even its new styling and the world's first production disc brakes didn't help. More often than not, the brakes corroded alarmingly when subjected to road salt and Crosley switched back to drums in 1950. A last ditch stand was the sporty Hotshot roadster which proved itself by winning the Index of Performance at the 1951 Sebring 12-Hour race and in standard tune could do 90 mph, a speed several larger cars of the day found hard to reach. It was Crosley's swan-song and by mid-1952, with only 2000 cars produced, company founder Powell Crosley called it quits and retired from the motoring scene.

Cadillac's supremacy of 1948 and 1949 was eclipsed by Chrysler in 1951, with the introduction of arguably the world's most advanced V-8 engine. It was the first V-8 ever produced by Chrysler and employed a hemispherical head combustion chamber. Chrysler's engineers had been working on various designs before settling on the legendary hemi configuration, chosen because it offered better volumetric efficiency, better cooling, a more central sparkplug location, and lower compression ratio allowing the use of lower octane fuel. While it displaced 331 cubic inches like Cadillac's engine, it developed 20-more horsepower than its rival and in stock trim, the short-stroke hemi at 180 hp was the most powerful engine on America's roads. 180 hp was only the tip of the iceberg; an early demonstration engine pumped out 352 hp but drag racers have been known to achieve 1000 hp from this masterpiece of engineering somewhat immodestly described as "the sensation of the century" in Chrysler advertising copy.

The hemi was first offered only on Chrysler New Yorker and Imperial models but DeSoto got a slightly smaller version in 1952, followed by Dodge in 1953. Dodge continued to offer the L-head six through 1958 but Chrysler and DeSoto were exclusively V-8 from 1954.

Sheetmetal shortages caused by the Korean war – any hopes that it would all be over by Christmas 1950 were soon dashed – found 1951 styling held over thru 1952, apart from minor trim changes to distinguish new models. Perhaps the most important news in the car industry was the stepping down of Chrysler president, K. T. Keller, in the fall of 1950 to be replaced by L. L. "Tex" Colbert. A significant catch for Chrysler was the hiring of stylist Virgil Exner and, between the two, Chrysler's image and market penetration made a complete turnaround. Over at Kaiser-Frazer the picture was far from promising. Sales were down badly in 1949, but a new 1951 Kaiser, introduced during 1950, pushed K-F from sixteenth to twelfth, overall. Differences of opinion between Kaiser and Frazer resulted in the latter leaving the company during 1951. Shortly after, the slow selling Frazer was dropped and replaced by the Henry J two-door compact.

New York's Fashion Academy selected the Henry J as the "Fashion Car of the Year" though nobody's quite sure why. A lot of people considered it downright ugly, including Howard "Dutch" Darrin, one of America's most talented stylists, and the guiding force behind the beautiful 1951 Kaiser. Company boss Henry J. Kaiser had chosen a design from American Metals Products which Darrin tried to improve on by adding a dip in the belt-line and adding vestigial fins at the rear.

For the 100″ wheelbase Henry J used Willys L-head four- and six-cylinder engines for its power, the little 134 cubic inch four giving over 30 mpg on a run while the 161 cubic inch six was quite a performer in the light, 2300 lb body, and was capable of zero to 60 in little over 14 seconds. Not quite hemi powered Chrysler performance but pretty good for an ancient design, nevertheless. Willing and able as the Henry J proved to be, its initial sales spurt (82,000 between September 1950 and December 1951) dropped to a trickle by the end of 1952 and it was downhill all the way until the end, in 1954.

After his Cadillac debut at Le Mans, Briggs Cunningham was encouraged enough to enter the 1951 race, this time using Chrysler Hemi engines in a car of his own design – the Cunningham C-2R. It took Cunningham and his team just three months to build, a miracle in itself and, although his three virtually untried cars didn't do all that well, at least one of the 300-hp cars held on to second place for six hours before making a meal of its valves. Of the remaining two, one spun off the course and the other, minus its connecting rod bearings, crawled home 18 places behind the winning Jaguar.

Not to be outdone, Cunningham returned to the fray in 1952 with a first at Elkhart and a first, second and fourth against all opposition at Watkins Glen. His new C-4R racers were 600 lbs. lighter and their mechanical modifications included roller tappet camshafts. At the race two cars were lost but Cunningham drove the surviving C-4R into fourth place after 19½ hours behind the wheel.

From 1953 to 1955, Cunningham built the C-3 grand touring sportscar for the general public. Coachwork for the coupe body was built by Michelotti of Italy while the frame and mechanicals were derived from the racing cars. Visually it was a stunning looker with power to match... it had to be, at $10,000 a car!

In 1953, Cunningham piloted the new C-5R to third place in the great French race and one of the team was timed at over 156 mph. A year later, two C-4Rs took third and seventh places, the best the marque would achieve but laudable nonetheless, considering the money spent on preparing and building the cars was insignificant compared to the factory supported teams. Cunningham almost pulled it off for America but it was to take Ford's millions to capture this, the most coveted motor racing prize, with its GT40s in 1966.

Hudson's stepdown design had been a great success and a new model, the Hornet, made its debut in 1951. Apart from a few trim differences, it looked much the same as other models but with an eye on the growing horsepower race, Hudson increased the displacement of its tough, six-cylinder powerplant to 308 cubic inches. It wasn't long before Hudson engineers realised they had a fierce performer on their hands and soon the NASCAR and AAA stock car races became Hudson domain. Race prepared Hudsons flattened the opposition, including the famed Olds 88, powering to victory no less than 27 times on NASCAR's ovals during 1952. One Hornet driver, Marshall Teague, finished 1000 points ahead of his nearest rival in the AAA championships.

Hudson's nearest competitor on the showroom floor was Nash. The companies were of similar size and both followed the unit construction school of thought. Nash, in fact, sold more cars than Hudson possibly because it had a wider range of models set on different wheelbases. The Ambassador, with its 121-inch wheelbase, was the largest. In 1950 the company, led by George Mason, introduced the 100" wheelbase Rambler American – America's first true post-war compact. A year later came the Anglo-American Nash-Healey two-passenger sports car powered by a hotter version of the Ambassador's six-cylinder engine. The Nash-Healey, built by Donald Healey in Britain, was both an attractive and competent handler and also very exclusive, if only by virtue of its very limited production run: from 1951 to 1955 when production ceased, fewer than 525 had been built.

Packard brought out all new models in 1951. The "pregnant elephant" design of 1948-1950 gave way to more attractive, smoother styling. The cheapest Packard, the 200 series, used a 122" wheelbase as did the more refined 250 while the 300 and 400 series were built on a 127" wheelbase. Top models had a 327 cubic inch eight, the lower orders a 288 cubic inch version.

Considered by many to be the styling *tour de force* of the 'fifties, there's no reason to doubt the 1953 Studebaker will go down as one of the best looking cars ever to hit the road. It is rare to find a car that is perfect from every angle with not a detail out of place, no line veering out of true. Designed by Robert E. Bourke of the famous Raymond Loewy Studios, the 1953 Studebaker, especially the two-door coupe models, should have outsold the competition over and over again. Sadly this was not to be the case; poor management, bad timing and pushing the four-door sedan instead of the lovely coupe everyone wanted, left Studebaker twiddling its thumbs with a disappointing 186,000 cars produced. Powered by a 232.6 cubic inch, 120 hp OHV V-8 introduced in 1951 (a six-cylinder engine was also available), the new Studebaker provided reliability as well as elegance at a price not much more than the somewhat dowdy Chevrolet of the same period. By the time Studebaker management sorted out model priorities it was too late. The customers lost patience and went elsewhere.

Even if they couldn't buy the Studebaker they wanted, shoppers weren't starved for choice. The major companies had re-styled or extensively facelifted their models with the exception of Ford, who had restyled the previous year. Unlike the 1949 thru '51 models, when a Ford was as distinctly different from a Mercury as the latter was from Lincoln, the 1952-53 cars bore a marked family resemblance to each other. This was especially true of Lincoln and Mercury but in no way detracts from the fact that the entire Ford range was handsome and made even handsomer with judicious trim modifications for 1953.

Lincoln was Ford's Cadillac chaser, a luxury car fitted out with power steering, power brakes and Hydramatic transmission as standard, and niceties such as electric windows, four-way power seat and air conditioning were desirable options. In 1952, Lincoln became the first Ford product to receive a brand new OHV V-8 to replace the ageing L-head. And to improve a first-rate quality car even further, Lincoln was the first to use ball-joint front suspension. Historically, Lincoln's major claim to fame during this period was its praiseworthy racing successes in the gruelling Carrera Panamerica road-race. It took the first five places in the International Standard Class in 1952, the first four in 1953 and one – two, in 1954.

Although Lincoln could be described as a better car, it harmed Cadillac's sales not one bit. Cadillac's undeniable reputation for quality and innovation was as old as the hills and the 1953 models were no exception. In the early 'fifties it was a joy to own a Cadillac, for styling changes were evolutionary rather than sudden. They were, with the exception of the later Eldorado Brougham, the best looking Cadillacs of the decade, the Coupe de Ville especially. Even if blessed with a certain risque opulence, a Cadillac looked authoritative and, like a chameleon, seemed able to adapt to fit in whatever surroundings it found itself in.

A car never short on presence during the 'forties and 'fifties, was Buick. One rung below Cadillac in GM's hierarchy, Buick always exuded a sort of conservative opulence favoured by many who preferred their glamor in subtle doses. "When Better Cars are Built, Buick will Build Them", went Buick ads. And Buick owners felt warm inside.

Buick decided to celebrate in style for 1953. After all, its 50th Anniversary was worth celebrating. Like Cadillac, Buick pursued a policy of evolutionary continuity and outwardly, the new models appeared little different from 1952. But Golden Anniversaries don't happen every year so Buick made the most of it with a brand new OHV V-8 engine and a special Anniversary model – the Skylark.

Borrowing from the custom car school, Buick's chief stylist, Ned Nickles and GM Head of Styling Harley Earl, took a Roadmaster convertible and chopped four inches off the windshield, lowered the belt-line and fashioned a notch behind the door – a styling ploy that made it on all Buicks the following year. To show off the expensive Kelsey Hayes wire wheels, the wheel arches were cut out. The result was a truly "Better Buick". It was also the most expansive, costing $5,000 or $1500 more than a standard Roadmaster convertible but came loaded with all the options, including leather upholstery and power everything as standard. The Skylark was offered only as a two-door convertible and was equipped with the new V-8.

With an 8.5:1 compression ratio, the highest in any American passenger car then available, the new, oversquare engine had a displacement of 322 cubic inches and developed 188 hp at 4000 rpm. It replaced the reliable old Fireball straight eight in all models but the lesser Special line, which retained the old engine until 1954.

Over at the Chevrolet end of GM's far-flung Empire something was stirring. Not on the normal lines which had all new styling as did Pontiac who shared the same Fisher "A" body shell, but on a brand new concept which had started out as a 1952 Motorama show car. Show cars were design exercises allowing designers and engineers to give vent to radical – and some not so radical – ideas for possible future use in production line vehicles. The best of these were shown at various motorshows at home and abroad to gauge public reaction to styling themes and engineering innovation. Chevrolet's 1952 show car was so successful and its design attractive, yet practical, that it appeared, with little alteration, on June 30th 1953, as the Corvette. It was the beginning of an era as the car became an instant legend every red-blooded American male aspired to, and a legend still in production today.

Responsibility for the birth of the Corvette lies with Harley Earl and Ed Cole, the latter a dynamic personality who became Chevrolet's chief engineer in 1952 (he eventually became GM president). Built of fiberglass, Earl had seen the advantages of producing cars in glass-reinforced plastic, the Corvette had a wraparound windshield, sunken headlamps protected by stone guards, and push button door handles. Under the hood, things were contemporary Chevy; the reliable, but in no way sporting, Blue Flame Six modified to produce 150 hp and Chevrolet's two-speed automatic transmission. Springs, shocks and steering were from Chevrolet's parts bin but adapted to give a more sportscar ride and feel.

Even with modifications, the Corvette disappointed sportscar connoisseurs – it just wasn't up to the standards of European sporting machinery, even though its 0-60 times were around 11 seconds and top speed in the region of 105 mph. Only 315 Corvettes were built the first year, partly because it was introduced very late in the season and the switch to 1954 production was only weeks away.

Oldsmobile and Cadillac also had special cars for 1953. Cadillac's was the costly ($7750) Eldorado convertible and Olds. fielded the Fiesta 98 convertible at a slightly more reasonable $5715. Both cars shared the dip in the belt-line aft of the doors *a la* Skylark but went one better than the latter by using wraparound windshields. All options were standard, including leather seating. Although described as "limited editions" it is doubtful GM meant them to be as limited as they were: only 458 Fiestas were produced as against 532 Eldorados and 1690 Skylarks. Buick built a watered down Skylark for 1954, producing under half the number of the previous year; the Fiesta didn't appear again but Cadillac stuck with the Eldorado in one form or another, right up to date.

Packard's special edition model was the glamorous Caribbean convertible priced at $5210. It came with all the good things in life as standard, had wire wheels and a remarkably chrome-free profile. Only 750 were produced but it outsold Cadillac's comparable model. Hudson, on the other hand, didn't go in for swank and introduced the compact Jet. The company wasn't doing so well and it hoped the $12 million investment in the Jet would solve some of its problems. The poor-selling Commodores were dropped but the, by now, out-dated Stepdown styling continued with the Hornet and the Wasp only because Hudson couldn't afford to restyle them. 21,143 Jets were produced, a total well below expectations. Not that it was a bad car; mechanically it was very sound and used Hudson's excellent six which gave the car creditable performance when fitted with the optional Twin H-Power set-up. Twin H-Power was offered in 1953 and comprised twin carburetors and dual manifold induction. The Jet then, should have sold; but it proved too unattractive and boxy for a consumer who wanted a bit more baroque.

Overall 1954 sales were down on the previous year but the worst affected were the independents and Chrysler. Plymouth, for so long the traditional No. 3 seller, dropped to fifth place with Buick moving up to take over the coveted spot. The reason was styling. Although Chrysler products were restyled in 1953, adopting one piece windshields and flow-thru fenders, they didn't look that much different from the uninspired 51/52 models. The same could be said for the '54s, hence the dramatic drop in sales.

By the time 1954 came around, all the independents were struggling. The immediate postwar sales boom signalled a prosperous future but circumstance wasn't with them. A lot of the troubles were of their own making; poor management, bad decisions and sometimes the wrong car for the time, all helped to bring them down. A terminal case if ever there was one, by 1954, was Kaiser. Another was Willys, a company who had been around since before the First World War and had led a pretty checkered career ever since. Willys had done well during WW II building Jeeps for the army. After hostilities had ended, Willys continued producing modified Jeeps for civilian use. Successful designer Brooks Stevens was contracted to come up with something a little more appealing, but still based on the Jeep. The result was the Jeepster convertible, a really rather smart vehicle ideally suited for western states and farming country. The 1948/49 models were powered by L-Head fours and sixes of 134 and 148 cubic inches, respectively. In the final two years of production, the Jeepster got an F-head four and the six was enlarged to 161 cubic inches.

In 1952, Willys introduced its first passenger car line since before the war. This was the Aero-Willys, a unit bodied car comprising four series; the Lark, Ace, Wing and Eagle. OHV and L-head sixes gave the nicely designed compacts 25 mpg and they remained in production until 1955. After production ended in America, the Willys continued to be made in Brazil, until 1962.

Before the end, Kaiser bought the company which became known as Kaiser-Willys Sales Corp. in 1953. It was a desperate move to try and consolidate their dwindling resources. About this time, Howard "Dutch" Darrin talked Kaiser into marketing a fiberglass bodied sportscar under his banner. Kaiser agreed and so was born the unique Kaiser-Darrin.

Due to the appalling state Kaiser-Willys found itself in, only 435 Kaiser-Darrins were built. It was an extraordinary car; we have all heard of gull-wing doors but the K-D went one better – it had sliding doors. These disappeared into a recess in the front fenders. Another interesting feature was a true landau top complete with genuine landau irons and like landau tops of old, could be set half or fully closed. The car had reasonable performance and could move along at almost 100 mph, thanks to its 90-hp Willys F-head six. This unusual and unique car only lasted one season before Kaiser-Willys put up the shutters in 1955.

Studebaker, Packard, Nash and Hudson reviewed their respective situations gloomily. They surmised they didn't have a dog's chance going it alone against the might of the Big Three who had millions of dollars to spend on new models…GM's budget alone was bigger than the GNP of some European countries. The Little Four decided there was only one practical course to take…they merged.

Merging did seem a good idea at the time and for one of the companies, American Motors, formed out of Hudson and Nash, it worked. Of the two, Nash was the healthier in pre-merger days probably because Nash-Kelvinator's president, George Mason, espoused small cars figuring it would pay rather than try

and compete with the big boys on their terms. Mason predicted that small cars would one day become an integral part of the American scene. Hence the 100-inch wheelbase Rambler in 1950. It, more than anything else, was responsible for Nash, then American Motors' survival.

The Rambler safely under his belt, Mason turned his attention to something even smaller. He and engineer Meade Moore, had been playing around with the idea since WW II. A prototype, styled by freelance designer Bill Flajole, was shown to the public in 1950. Reaction was favorable as were the results of a questionnaire handed out to the public wherever the prototype was shown. Financial estimates decreed it would be more economical to have the car, code named NXI (Nash Experimental International), assembled in Europe. A couple of companies were approached but in the end the contract for producing NXI went to Austin of England.

NXI became the Metropolitan and went on sale in 1954. Looking for all the world like a truncated Nash Ambassador, the little Metropolitan caused quite a stir. Engine and drivetrain were modified Austin A40 but front and rear suspension were Rambler "Deep Coil" units linked to British Girling direct action shocks.

George Mason died in early October, 1954 and George Romney, later a Governor of Michigan, became president. Like Mason before him, Romney was wedded to small cars and he took American Motors from strength to strength, but not without some severe pruning, as we will shortly see.

If American Motors merger worked well, the opposite occurred with the Studebaker-Packard alliance. The real problem was Studebaker which was deep into the red, but Packard president James J. Nance didn't realise this until after he bought the South Bend company.

With the exception of Ford there was little change in the big camps over 1953. Buick, Olds and Cadillac got new grilles, wraparound windshields and horsepower increases and Buick showed off the radical, experimental Wildcat II. Ford stole a march on Chevrolet and Plymouth when it introduced its new OHV Y-block V-8 rated at 130 hp. Mercury's version was bigger and developed 161 hp. Both cars shared a new ball-joint front suspension system. Styling changes were minimal but Ford and Mercury added a new model to their respective line-ups. Ford had the Crestline Skyliner, Mercury the Monterey Sun Valley. These were distinguished by a clear, tinted plastic sun-roof. Hardtops were increasing in popularity – both the Skyliner and Sun Valley were hardtop models – and had been ever since Buick marketed the first production hardtop in its Riviera series, in 1949. Actually, credit for the first hardtop belongs to Chrysler, who showed a prototype Town and Country hardtop in 1946. Strangely, the car never went into production.

1955 was the sort of year auto makers look back upon and wistfully declare: "Aah! Those were the days". Taking into account the problems the industry has suffered over the past few years, who can blame them? Everything in the garden was coming up roses and the new cars reflected the nation's *joie de vivre*.

Ford and Chevy had been battling it out for some time but during the 'fifties the war had hotted up. The prize was the number one slot in the sales charts and Ford was determined to wrest the position away from Chevrolet. By 1955 Ford had closed the gap considerably.

The newly designed Fords were very attractive cars featuring the now fashionable "dog-leg"…as some road testers described wraparound windshields, a full width, concave lattice grille, peaked headlights and a sweep spear running from atop the fenders, kinking at the door, then running the length of the car. This unusual, but graceful styling ploy accentuated Ford's pleasing two-tone color schemes available on the top Fairlane range. Ford's lowest priced series, the Mainline Tudor and Fordor sedans, had little in the way of chrome embellishments and were regarded as salesmen's hacks.

A new model was the Fairlane Crown Victoria distinguished by a swatch of chrome starting at the rear door pillar and arching over the roof and down the other side. It rather gave the impression of a basket handle and only lasted two seasons. The Crestline Skyliner became the Crown Victoria Skyliner, its transparent top separated by the odd chrome basket handle.

The big news in the Ford camp was the Thunderbird, Dearborn's belated answer to the Corvette. Coyly termed a "personal car" – Ford rightly declined describing it as a sportscar – the Thunderbird was one of the most beautiful models ever to come out of a car factory *anywhere*. Even though its mechanical parts and some body pieces were interchangeable with regular Fords the T-Bird had perfect symmetry of line. Almost 30 years on it still doesn't look out of date.

Horsepower was way up on nearly every American-produced car and the T-Bird was no exception. The regular Fords had been bored out to 272 cubic inches but the T-bird displaced 292 cubic inches and developed 193 hp. A T-Bird buyer could load his car with all the available options including electric windows, air conditioning, PAS, power brakes and Fordomatic transmission.

Arch-rival Chevrolet had quite a bit to offer as well. Everything was brand-new including the engine. Stylewise, Chevy's 14 models were the best looking for years. Lower, beautifully proportioned and featuring a latticework grille reminiscent of Ferrari, the 1955 Chevrolets were arguably the looks champions of the low price field. They featured wraparound windshields, 20 new two-tone color combinations and, for the first time in 35 years, a new V-8.

The new V-8, displacing 265 cubic inches, was rated at 165 hp. It was designed by Ed Cole and engineer Harry F. Barr. It had a compact bore and stroke of 3.75 × 3, five main bearings and its wedge shaped combustion chambers were fed by a dual throat carburetor. A power package, including a four barrel set-up, increased hp to 180. Christened "Turbo-Fire", Chevrolet's engine was so efficient that it was one of the greatest power plants the world had seen and is still recognised as such. One car that really benefited was the Corvette – the V-8 transformed its image overnight and probably saved the little sportscar from extinction.

Over at Chrysler, Virgil Exner's "$100 Million Dollar Look" had arrived. After years of dull uninspired designs, the new cars were a complete break with the past. From Chrysler to Plymouth, Exner had transformed them from ugly ducklings to beautiful swans. The big Chryslers and Imperial – now a separate make in its own right – were the best looking. Two-speed Powerflite automatic, first available on 1954 models, was standard on New Yorker and Imperial models, optional on other lines. Unusual was the selector location on the instrument panel. Everything from power windows to seats and air conditioning were available.

Since its introduction in 1951, hemi-powered Chryslers had made a good showing of themselves in various forms of automotive competition. This experience proved invaluable and resulted in one of the greatest cars of the decade – the 1955 Chrysler C-300. The brainchild of Chrysler's chief engineer Bob Rodger and stylist Virgil Exner, the 300 was put together inside six months. The main ingredients were already there and it was a matter of somebody putting them together.

Exner took a New Yorker body, dechromed it and added the larger Imperial split grille to the front end. The interior was redesigned and seating covered in hand stiched leather. Only three exterior colors were used: Platinum white, black and Tango red.

For his part, Rodger took the standard hemi 331 c.i.d. block, fitted solid valve lifters and an additional four barrel carburetor, among other things. The engine developed 300 hp, hence the car's name. Stiffer shocks and springs were used all round. Options were few; Kelsey Hayes wire wheels, PAS, clock, radio, electric windows, tinted glass and power seats was about all that was available. But the result was America's only true Grand Touring car and a spectacular one at that.

It wasn't long before the 300 went racing, much to the consternation of its rivals. It dominated everything it entered and at the end of the season had captured all three major stock car championships, becoming the first car ever to do so. First it clinched Daytona's Speed Week trials, breaking records along the way, taking the Flying Mile at well over 127 mph, qualified for the 160-mile Daytona Grand National at over 130 mph and took the race itself at an average of 92.05 mph. Driven by some of the best race drivers in the business, C-300s took 37 first places out of 52 races entered, clinching the NASCAR and AAA championships. Although only 1725 C-300s were built (136 remain today) its image rubbed off on the standard Chryslers, giving the division its second best sales year since the marque first appeared 31 years earlier.

Dodge more than doubled production over 1954, hardly surprising when comparisons are made between the new styling and the old. An improved hemi Red Ram engine developing 175 hp, with Powerflite transmission, two inches lopped off the body height and 16 inches additional length gave Dodge its best year since 1951 which would not be surpassed until 1960. Plymouth, on the other hand, hasn't since improved on its 1955 total of 742,991 which broke all previous records but still not quite enough to dislodge Buick from third place. Besides attractive new styling, Plymouth fielded its first V-8. The new "Hy-Fire" engine had aluminium pistons, aluminium carburetor and a polyspherical combustion chamber. In its wildest tune the OHV engine developed 177 hp and for excellence was regarded in almost the same breath as Chevrolet's example.

Clever restyling gave Packard's old body an entirely new look for 1955. A little on the garish side but impressive nonetheless, the idea was to recapture the luxury image which had been watered down with the production of low-priced cars.

Besides new styling, and turning the cheaper Clipper into a separate make, Packard offered a host of advanced technological features including Torsion-Level suspension. This consisted of nine-foot long torsion bars interconnected to all four wheels, thus eliminating conventional springs. A complicated system of smaller torsion bars connected to a compensator gear box, electrically controlled, automatically kept the car at even keel, regardless of road conditions or increases and decreases of weight distribution. The combination of torsion bars and level control gave Packard excellent handling and ride properties superior to most.

Other important Packard features included an all-new engine and an improved Twin-Ultramatic transmission. The 352 cubic inch V-8 was the largest to be found in any passenger car and had a torque rating of 355 lb-ft at 2400-2800 rpm. On the top line 400 and Caribbean models, PAS, power brakes, automatic transmission and four-way power seats were standard fare but available options included air conditioning – a Packard first, by the way, Packard had offered air conditioning back in 1940.

Studebaker entered its third year with the Loewy/Bourke body but ruined it with an over-ornate and heavy front end. Over at the newly formed American Motors, Nash adapted a wraparound windshield and inboard headlights to its '54 styling and clever sheet-metal work made a Hudson out of Nash's unitized body. In an agreement with Studebaker-Packard, AMC used Packard engines and transmissions as an alternative to the standard six-cylinder mills.

Buick, Oldsmobile, Mercury, Lincoln and Cadillac contented themselves with more horsepower and minor alterations. Buick lost its teeth and got a wide mesh grille instead.

Undoubtedly, Thunderbird, Chrysler's C-300, Chevrolet and Packard were the standouts in one of the most exciting years in American automotive history. Sales broke all records with 7,943,274 cars produced. Bristling with innovations and color, they were the right cars at the right time.

After the excitement of 1955 the industry looked to 1957 and beyond for a repeat performance. In most quarters 1956 was relagted to minor facelifts here and there; for instance, Chevrolet tacked on a full width grille and the rest of GM did more of less the same. Chrysler, Dodge, De Soto and Plymouth concentrated on horsepower and grille changes; but more apparent were the fins each model was cultivating.

Ford and Mercury left well enough alone but Lincoln, who hadn't had a new model in '55, got it for 1956. Seven inches longer, three inches wider, the new Lincoln looked like nothing that went before. The design was clean and reasonably unadorned save for a chrome molding on the lower half of the body. Headlights were recessed in a deep, peaked shroud, wheel openings were partially covered and the obligatory wraparound windshield closed the door on the relatively conservative Lincolns of the past.

Ever since Ford dispensed with the classic Continental, dealers had been clamoring for its return. Bowing to their wishes Ford set up a separate division to produce a new Continental so perfect that it would set a precedent for any cars competing in the high price field. Announced as the Continental Mark II it stole the show for 1956.

Henry Ford II's younger brother, William Clay Ford, was head of The Special Products Division responsible for the Mark II's design. Various outside stylists were asked to submit ideas but in the end it was Special Products team of stylists who won the day. It consisted of John Reinhart, Bob Thomas and great artist Gordon Buehrig, he was the designer of the fabulous Cord 810/812 so it was hardly surprising that their design was chosen over all others.

The keynote of the Mk. II's design was simplicity. Some might even call it severe but its long hood, short deck theme anticipated a movement in that direction during the late 'sixties. Its simple, honeycomb grille, interrupted by five slender vertical bars, owed much to European design but the Continental rear tire cover was pure American and a throw-back to the previous Continental.

Mechanically the Continental was fairly conventional and used Lincoln's 368 cubic inch engine. Following Rolls-Royce's lead the Continental Division was coy about horsepower figures, deeming them to be "adequate". All equipment that was optional on lesser breeds came as standard on the Continental, which cost close on $10,000. That was a lot of money in those days but anybody fortunate enough to be able to afford it got his money's worth. Each engine was individually selected and tested, all materials checked for close tolerances and each car given a 12-mile road test. It took four times the labor content to produce a Continental than a standard Lincoln and quality was readily apparent. From its styling to its finish the Continental was a match for Rolls and Bentley. And whereas many cars of the period are hopelessly dated, a Mark II is timeless enough to fit in a current setting with aplomb.

The Continental, in common with all Ford products, stressed safety for 1956. Mindful of a growing outcry against the horsepower race Ford elected to show it had the consumers' interests at heart and was one of the first to include safety features in all its cars. Buying a Ford product meant having a deep dished collapsible steering wheel, shatterproof rear mirror, safety door-locks, padded instrument panel shelf and optional seat belts. The company played safety for all it was worth in its advertising but met with an unsympathetic response from the consumer, who seemed to prefer performance to safety.

As 1957 approached everyone hoped it would be better than 1956. Eisenhower was back for a second term but good times on the home front were shaken by the Suez Crisis and the Hungarian Uprising. The nation's youth were more interested in a young man from Tupelo: Elvis had a series of chart hits beginning with "Heartbreak Hotel" and, much to the despairing parents' alarm, rock 'n' roll was here to stay. GM appreciated Presley, though; he'd bought a couple of Cadillacs, the one painted pink, he gave to his mother.

World problems and Elvis were soon forgotten when unveiling time for the 1957 cars came around. Of the three major manufacturers only GM relied on a face-lift – and an extensive one at that. Judging by collector interest, songs featuring it and general nostalgia for it, the '57 Chevrolet undoubtedly came off best. Conservative compared to the all-new Ford and Plymouth, Chevrolet sold 1.5 million cars, nonetheless.

The new Chevy sported a massive oval bumper/grille combination with a gold or silver colored mesh insert. Headlights were peaked and twin chrome windsplits decorated either side of the hood. At the rear, slender chrome-capped fins balanced the overall effect. Outstanding was its 283 cubic inch V-8 developing 283 hp – one horsepower per cubic inch. Chevrolet also offered a GM designed fuel injection system which was also available on the Corvette, now recognised as a true sportscar since Zora Arkus-Duntov took over the car's development in 1955. Duntov threw away the anemic six cylinder engine and dropped a V-8 in the redesigned '56 'Vette which became a potent force to be reckoned with. The '57 model with a fuel injected 283 could really fly!

When Semon E. Knudsen, known to his friends as "Bunky", took over as general manager of Pontiac in 1956, a wind of change swept over the staid Aunt Agatha cars. Under Knudsen's guidance, Pontiac became hot performance cars, especially the Bonneville making its first appearance in 1957. With 310 hp under its hood and fuel injection or Tri-Power (three two-barrel carbs.), the Bonneville blew the dusty Pontiac image out the window. It wasn't to be long before Pontiac became the car to beat, on road or track.

As far as GM's other divisions were concerned, 1957 was a case of longer, lower, wider and mountains of chrome gimmickry. Cadillac didn't follow this route entirely but came up with an extensive restyle. The Eldorado Biarritz and Seville were particularly attractive, boasting a tail treatment entirely different from the regular models. The tail was rounded and sloped down to meet the bumper and an unusual but novel styling feature were the inboard mounted, shark-like fins. Up front the hood was flatter, a feature common to all models and the wraparound windshield wrapped further into a point, a piece of styling questionable to say the least and a real safety hazard as many who have suffered near knee-cappings, would tell you.

Cadillac hadn't taken Ford's reintroduction of the Continental lying down and countered with the ultra expensive Eldorado Brougham in 1957. At over $13,000 it pipped the Continental by $3000 but the fortunate few able to afford it got a lot more for their money. Borrowing heavily from various Harley Earl Cadillac dream cars, the Eldorado's styling didn't achieve the classic elegance of the Continental. Its kinship with regular Cadillacs was unmistakable and its very closeness to its lesser brethren might have spoiled its distinctive appeal.

Whatever the arguments over the Brougham's styling, it was, without doubt, a fine car. It was crammed to its unique brushed stainless steel roof with innovations, many lifted straight from the show cars. Unlike the Continental, the Eldorado was a pillarless four-door hardtop with the doors opening from the center and locking in sturdy 14-inch posts when closed. Everything was power operated including the trunk lid and its six-way power front seat had a memory setting. As the driver opened the door, the seat would slide back to allow easy exit. On re-entering, the seat automatically moved back to the selected position.

GM had been experimenting with various types of air suspension and the Eldorado Brougham was fitted with Cadillac's version. The system comprised four rubber air bags located at each wheel instead of the

springs. An air compressor combined with an accumulator, levelling valves and solenoid controls, activated the suspension. This complex bag of tricks was meant to give a superior ride and keep the car at a constant level at all times. Which it did when it worked – trouble was, more often than not it didn't and many owners converted their Broughams to conventional coils. GM continued to offer air suspension of one form or another but had so many problems that the idea was shelved after 1959.

Chrysler and Ford stole a march on mighty GM with totally new styling across the board, save the Continental and regular Lincolns, the latter which contented itself with the addition of canted fins. The entire Chrysler Corp. line-up was a revolution on wheels, thanks to Virgil Exner's radical, yet beautifully proportioned, designs. From Chrysler to Plymouth the slogan was "Suddenly its 1960" which confused a lot of people who thought it was still 1957, so it was changed to "…Three Years Ahead".

Exner's designs were dramatic because his fins, started in a small way the year before, had come of age. They graced the smooth, flowing lines, flat hoods, and huge, sharply swept back panoramic windshields with a look of motion even when the cars were standing still. Each division was given its own personality: Dodge was colorful but aggressive; Chrysler and Imperial graceful and free of over decoration; Plymouth, aggressive without the Dodge brashness while De Soto was somewhere in the middle.

It wasn't just styling that made Chrysler cars the ones to beat. They had an entirely new suspension system. Not to be confused with Packard's all round torsion bar system, Chrysler's Torsion-Aire utilised torsion bars on the front only. The rear suspension was conventional leaf springs modified for better handling. And as far as handling went, 1957 Chrysler products were top of the league; they cornered flatter, sopped up road irregularities with less dive and squat, leading some observers to enthusiastically remark that the cars handled better than some European sportscars!!!

Exner's finny styling theme was arguably carried off best by the machismo orientated 300-C. Its unique trapezoid shaped grille bearing a degree of Italian influence put on an aggressive front to the flowing lines of the car. Large horizontal air scoops housed beneath the dual headlights served to cool the large brakes, an area much neglected by U.S. car makers at the time. To haul the 375 hp or optional 390 hp car down, it needed good brakes!!

Although the 300-C was fast and furious it didn't go racing like its illustrious forebears, the C-300 and 300-B. Carl Kiekhaefer, president of Mercury Outboard Motors and 300 racing team sponsor, withdrew from competition at the end of the '56 season following disagreement over NASCAR's rules policies. Then the American Manufacturers' Association banned auto makers from competition mainly to allay fears of the consumer, who equated high horsepower with high insurance rates.

Plymouth's dazzling '57 styling had achieved Chrysler's low priced division's immediate ambition – to regain third place from Buick. This it did with gusto and Chrysler Corp. ended the year with 19.5% of the overall market, mostly at the expense of GM. And to rub salt into GM's wounds even further, the newly styled Fords came within an ace of beating Chevy to No. One. Whether they actually *did* succeed is still a matter of debate for the difference in numbers produced by either side amounted to 130 cars. As far as Ford cars go they should have won. They were three to four inches lower, wider, came on two wheelbases of 116 and 118 inches and, in the case of the Fairlane series, were nine inches longer than the '56 models, and very handsome.

Ford offered a wide choice of engines in its 21 model line-up: from a 144 hp six to a wild supercharged 300 hp V-8. Standard mill in the Fairlanes was a 212 hp V-8, 202 in the cheaper Custom series. Two brand new models made their debut for 1957. One was the amazing Fairlane Skyliner Hardtop complete with a retractable steel roof. Oddly, it was Ford's least popular model and lasted only three years. Far more acceptable was the Ranchero Pickup. Quite unlike the pickups of previous years, the Ranchero was a car with a pickup bed. It offered all the luxuries one would expect on a regular auto and was trimmed like the station wagons. Sales were brisk and had the Ranchero figured in the final production tally, then Chevrolet was well and truly beaten in 1957.

1957 was the final year for the two-place Thunderbird and probably the most attractive of all. The following year Ford brought out a larger four-seater T-Bird that was *kitsch* by comparison. Not that this mattered to the public who bought twice as many T-Birds than in 1957.

Two respected names died as American Motors administered the *coup de grace* to Hudson and Nash. The 1957 versions of these two famous marques were not the prettiest but they had bags of honest quality and character. This left AMC to concentrate on the Rambler. Since its smart restyling in 1956, the

Rambler was a healthy seller and the savior of AMC. A popular model was the station wagon; the least popular the Rebel hardtop. A complete contradiction to Rambler's normal, economic self, the Rebel had a 327 cubic inch V-8, special suspension and 0 to 60 mph in fractionally over seven seconds. Only 1500 or so were made and if any survivors can be found, it is a worthwhile collector's car today.

Over at Studebaker-Packard things could hardly have been worse. Sales were down by 7000 on 1956's derisory total of 80,000 odd. Not that Studebaker/Packard weren't producing good cars; they were. The last Loewy designed Studebaker Hawk series, based n the '53-'55 body, was a beautiful creation. There were four Hawk models; the Power, Flight, Sky and the Golden Hawk which was the top of the tree. The smallest was the six-cylinder Flight Hawk but the big 352 cubic inch Packard V-8 provided the Golden Hawk with plenty of get up and go. With no money to go anywhere, S/P reduced the 1957 Hawk series to the Golden Hawk and the new Silver Hawk which was an amalgam of the rest. Minor face-lifting confined itself to the addition of canted fins and trim alterations.

For all its innovation, the '55/'56 Packards didn't sell, partly because all the bugs hadn't been ironed out before the cars went on sale. Packard struggled into 1957 as a glorified Studebaker but was different enough to distinguish the two. Not so in 1958 when little attempt was made to disguise the fact that the final Packard was a Studebaker with knobs on...a Packebaker, if you like. Studebaker-Packard tried to make a Packard Hawk by grafting on a hideous fiberglass nose to the Golden Hawk and succeeded in giving the car a more than passing resemblance to the Creature from the Black Lagoon. One of the finest names in motoring had been consigned to the history books. People still regret its passing and hindsight tells us it need never have happened. Had Packard stayed on its own and concentrated on limited runs of high quality cars, the sort of vehicles it was used to building, there's every reason to believe it would still be with us today.

A mini recession clouded the American landscape during 1958 and car sales were the first to suffer. Production tumbled right across the board with a calendar year total of 4,049,829, almost half the 1955 figure. Perhaps the public acted wisely by not investing in new cars; what they got in return was pretty awful!

After a successful year, Chrysler hung on to what it had got for 1958 with only minor alterations to trim and grilles. It was a terrible year for Chrysler who suffered the most out of the Big Three. The company still had the best looking cars but had an unenviable reputation of shoddy workmanship inherited from 1957. Quality control was tightened up during 1958 but the stigma remained.

General Motors got a touch of the sun when designing their new models. Universally regarded as the ugliest designs ever to come our of Detroit, GM's '58 crop were heavy handed barges with more chrome than was probably available in Rhodesia's (now Zimbabwe) mines. Buick and Oldsmobile were the worst offenders with chrome plate piled on wherever possible. Of GM's 1958 cars only Chevrolet, over-decorated as it was, managed anything approaching good looks.

If anybody managed to get it right and wrong in the same year, it was Ford. Right was the '58 four-passenger Thunderbird selling almost twice as many cars as the previous year's classic twoseater, and wrong – and Ford really bombed on this one – was the $250 million Edsel fiasco.

To be fair, the Edsel was quite a good car albeit a very ugly one. Had it been marketed two, maybe three years earlier, when medium priced cars commanded 25-35% of the total sales, it would have done very well. Unfortunately the recession and a change in public tastes effected this end of the market.

The Edsel was designed by Ford stylist, Roy A. Brown, and came in four series, the lower priced Ranger and Pacer sharing the Ford Fairline body, the costlier Corsair and Citation using Mercury's body shell. Wheelbases were 118 and 124 inches respectively. The small models used a 361 cubic inch V-8 and a 410 c.i.d. engine powered the larger versions.

The striking thing about the Edsel and still a subject of debate, even today, was its narrow upright grille. A butt of many jokes, the vertical format was dubbed a horse collar by the kindly although sucked lemon and even cruder descriptions were used by the not so beneficent. Horizontal gullwing tail-lights decorated the rear and were about the only other unconventional touch on an otherwise very "normal" car.

With great fanfare the Edsels were launched on September 4th 1957 and first public reaction was one of disappointment. From all the pre-publicity hype the public had hoped for something special and a horse-collar grille on a conventional car wasn't their idea of a radical new style. It didn't take Ford long to realise the Edsel was a mistake; to break even in its first year Ford needed to sell around 150,000 cars; as it

was, only 65,212 found homes between September 1957 and December 1958.

One of the weaknesses of the motor industry is its inability to accurately gauge public tastes three years ahead. The Edsel is a good case in point; to design and tool up for a new car takes three years, so by the time it hits the market chances are the consumers want something entirely different. A good example of change occurred in 1959...people were fed up with over-ornate behemoths and were looking to the smaller foreign cars. And the only American auto to post increased sales in 1958 had been the compact Rambler...

After the garish '58 models and consequent poor sales, it's hardly surprising GM rushed out entirely new 1959 cars. What is surprising is the cars bore little or no relationship to what went before.

The changes were dramatic right across the board. Only Corvette stayed the same. Buick, once the grand old lady with a solid, conservative reputation had undergone a metamorphosis so complete that even the names of the various models had been changed. They were lower, but not longer, with canted front fenders flowing smoothly into the body. Rear canted fins started at the front doors and swept gracefully to the rear. Like all cars in 1959, the windshield wrapped over the top as well as round. In common with all other GM models the four-door hardtops had a huge panoramic rear screen wrapping round to the rear door edge. 56 little chrome cubes made up the full width grille but the tail-lights were simple convex discs inserted in a band of chrome.

The top Electra and Invicta models got a new 401 cubic inch engine but the lower priced LeSabre remained with the older 364 cubic inch mill. The unreliable air suspension was still available but on the rear wheels only.

Adopting the same policy as the other big companies, GM had two basic bodies shared between the divisions. Looking closely at any of the cars, be it Oldsmobile or Pontiac, inner and outer panel similarities become self evident. True badge engineering, thankfully hadn't entered the picture and each division was able to individualise its product through styling differences. Body sharing and the use of the same mechanical components had its advantages, the major one being lower production costs.

Of the rest of GM's cars, Oldsmobile had what can only be described as oval fins but Chevrolet's were the most outrageous. It had huge cats-eye chrome framed tail-lights topped by gullwing shaped fins and was 11 inches longer than the '57 model, with the same engine options as before.

Pontiac was the wild one for 1959. It was the year of the first twin split grilles which became a Pontiac trademark. More important was Pontiac's much ballyhooed Wide-Track. This consisted of widening the tread a full five inches thereby enhancing handling and ride immeasurably and also ensuring the division Motor Trend magazine's coveted Car of the Year award.

Of all GM's 1959 products, Cadillac was the most garish. Obviously its space-age styling was inspired by Sputniks and John Glenn and it had skyscraper fins larger than even Chrysler's worst excesses. It shunned Buick's little chrome cubes for 126 chrome button like protruberences. Cadillac got a new 390 cubic inch engine developing up to 345 hp. For such a great white whale the car handled pretty well, thanks to suspension modifications and better power steering. The new Eldorado Biarritz...not to be mistaken for the luxuriant Eldorado Brougham that ceased production in 1958...was the fleetest, best looking '59 model. All '59 Cadillacs are highly collectible, today.

Chrysler had dropped their hemi for more conventional wedge engines, due to cost more than any-thing. The new engines put out gobs of power and didn't take a back seat to anyone, but purists bemoaned the loss of the hemi in the 300 Letter Series.

Styling changes were restricted to grilles and trim but all models offered a curious oval steering wheel and swivel front seats. As is usual with a three year old body, styling alterations tend to spoil the original lines and nowhere was this more evident than at Chrysler. Still, the public liked what it saw and all Chrysler divisions showed increased sales over 1958.

Like Chrysler, Ford stuck to its 1957 body shell but extensively restyled so successfully that it captured the number one spot from Chevrolet by a handsome margin. For once the styling was better at the end of the cycle than at the beginning. And to prove the point, Ford picked up an award for design excellence at the Brussels (Belgium) World Fair.

It was to be the last year for the none too popular Fairlane 500 Skyliner Retractable hardtop. Sales had never been good but it was the only Ford to post a decrease in 1959. Fun car it was, an expression of the rock 'n' roll era and a technical marvel. Unfortunately, with the roof stowed away in the trunk there was nowhere to put any luggage. Added to the fact that it cost more than, say, a Ford Sunliner convertible which had the advantage of trunk space, buyers were put off. Only 12,915 Skyliners left the factory in 1959, hardly enough to justify Ford continuing its production.

Little imported cars were beginning to make their presence sorely felt by 1959 as more people turned away from some of Detroit's excesses. Only two American manufacturers were building compacts, AMC with its Rambler, and Studebaker had entered the fray with the introduction of the Lark. Essentially the Lark was a scaled down, full-size Studebaker, yet stylist Duncan McRae had performed an excellent job in making the Lark appear new.

Powered by either a six or eight cylinder engine, the Lark was a great success and for the first time in six years Studebaker actually made a profit on a total of 150,000 cars including the Hawks. It was the same story over at AMC; sales of its cars moved the company into the top ten. Small cars were selling like hot cakes and it wasn't long before the big guns zeroed in for a slice of what was rapidly turning into a profitable market.

As the final minutes of 1959 ticked away they were taking with them one of the most extraordinary periods in U.S. automotive history. Stylists had come into their own and the results of their labors were often spectacular, if not always in the best of taste. Then again, who would have thought a car like the Chrysler 300, the Continental Mk. II or the Chevy Nomad would have come along? The 'fifties spawned other great cars and whatever anyone says, there can be no doubt it was one of the most imaginative periods of all time.

America drove into the 'sixties in a new type of car. The Big Three compacts had arrived; Valiant from Chrysler, Corvair and Falcon from GM and Ford respectively. In a way it was like going back to 1950; the compacts were as different from each other as chalk is from cheese. And they weren't that much smaller than the 1950 low-priced three – it was only that the latter had grown so big over the succeeding years.

Of the three, Chevrolet's Corvair was a technological wonder. It had an aluminium opposed air-cooled six cylinder engine at the rear (like Volkswagen), four wheel independent suspension and unique styling. Ford's Falcon was just the opposite and utterly conventional with an OHV six up front and looked what it was...a down sized Ford. The Valiant, on the other hand, had a very European look to it and was styled by Virgil Exner. Its mechanical side was similar to the Falcon.

Both Ford and Chrysler pooh-poohed the Corvair for its rear mounted engine in their advertising. "The engine's up front", shouted Ford in praise of the Falcon, "to reduce the chance of oversteering (characteristic of many rear engine cars)...". Ford also sneakily claimed the Falcon's hot water heater "eliminates fumes and danger of gasoline fueled heater inside the car (required by air-cooled cars)". Of course Corvair countered this with its own insults. The war was on...who would win?

The Falcon won hands down. It sold almost twice as many cars as the other two put together. In those days folk still tended to be suspicious of anything different. Perhaps they had a premonition of the troubles that were soon to come Corvair's way – troubles in the guise of Ralph Nader.

1960's sales were way up on 1959 and the compacts, including Lark and Rambler, accounted for well over a million units. That was almost 20% of total sales, and encouragement enough for the Big Three to hustle out five new models the following year. There was the Buick Special powered by a 215 cubic inch aluminium V-8 (eventually sold to British Leyland to use in its Rover), Oldsmobile's F-85 Cutlass with the same engine and the radical Pontiac Tempest.

The Tempest used a 195 cubic inch four as its base engine but its curved drive shaft and transaxle were new for a Detroit car. The system worked well but in 1964 the Tempest switched to a conventional layout.

The other two entries in the compact field were the Dodge Lancer and Mercury Comet. The Lancer shared everything with the Valiant apart from the grille and trim but the Comet, though sharing Falcon's body, differed considerably.

GM had second thoughts about its big car lines and toned down their radical '59 styling by softening the lines and removing much of the chrome. Ford came out with all new styling, apeing Chevrolet's gullwing rear, but in more subdued fashion. It also dispensed with the controversial dogleg windshield, taking a leaf out of Chrysler's book and adapting a slant back curved screen. The gargantuan Lincoln and Continental – the Mark II died in 1957 – were to continue for another year. As for Mercury it also remained much the same as 1959.

With the exception of the Imperial, all Chrysler products had unitized body-chassis construction for 1960. These were Virgil Exner's last styling exercises for Chrysler and the famous fins soared just a little higher, especially on the new Plymouth and Imperial; both ugly cars. There was a death in the family – after many years of declining sales, DeSoto perished shortly after the '61 models appeared. It wasn't alone because the ailing Edsel was finally put down by Ford after only 2846 cars had been built.

Robert MacNamara, Ford's group vice-president of car divisions, dropped by the styling studio one day and saw several full size clay mock-ups round the room. One in particular took his fancy...it was a proposal for the 1961 T-Bird. Looking at it for a while, MacNamara stepped back and said it would be much better as the new Continental. And so it was done; the clay evolved into the 1961 Continental and, like the 1956/57 Mk II, became an instant classic.

It was a beautiful car, even better than the Mark II. Its lines were smooth and without embellishment. Apart from the honeycomb grille with inset dual headlights and bumper, the only ornamentation were stainless steel fender strips running the car's full length. Power was delivered by a 300 hp V-8 and each engine was dynamometer tested for three hours, taken apart for inspection, reassembled and rechecked again on a 12-mile road test in the finished automobile.

The Continental's seven-man team of designers won the Industrial Designers Institute's annual award for design. It also won immediate public acceptance with sales of over 25,000 in its first year. This was compared to sales of under 25,000 for the 12-model 1960 Lincoln and Continental; the 1961 fielded three models as Lincoln Continentals only. A specially built Continental limousine was delivered to the White House for President Kennedy's use on Affairs of State – it was also the car he used on that fateful day in Dallas, two years later.

The public's mood toward conservatism was increasingly reflected in automobile design. Chrysler finally shed its fins in 1962 and sales jumped 20,000 over 1961 as a result. Much to the purists' chagrin, Chrysler dropped the Windsor name and re-christened the car 300. The famed Letter Series, now the 300H, continued as the grand tourer.

Exner had already designed all Chrysler products up to 1964 but from 1965 models to 1969 car design was Elwood Engle's responsibility. Engle had been the main motivator behind the successful Continental's styling and was quite a catch for Chrysler.

1961 and 1962 GM cars had been restyled and were far more attractive than anything put out by them since 1958. The flamboyant windshields were gone as were fins and unnecessary chrome embellishments. Horsepower, which had remained pretty static, was beginning to creep up again from 1962. Chevrolet offered a massive 409 cubic inch, fuel injected engine rated at 409 hp – as with the famous 283, one hp per cubic inch. At the other end of the scale was the new Chevy II Nova compact with either a 153 cubic inch four-cylinder or a six-cylinder engine of 194 c.i.d. The Nova was rushed out to try to staunch the flow of buyers heading toward Ford dealerships and the Falcon. The Corvair was a non-runner against the reliable Falcon but was preferred by sporty car enthusiasts, particularly the 1962 Monza Spyder model with its 150 hp turbocharged flat six engine.

Buyer interest was swinging more and more to performance and Detroit was quick to satisfy the growing need. Younger buyers had more money than ever before and it was at this large segment the sportier cars were aimed. Buick trotted out the 325 hp Wildcat, Oldsmobile turbocharged an F-85 and called it the Jetfire.

Performance may have been the coming thing but there were enough people still wanting reliable, economical transportation. Rambler did spectacularly well in the early 'sixties, cheekily grabbing third place from Plymouth two years in a row. Dodge and Plymouth's standard lines had grown smaller in '62 and suffered as a result of unorthodox styling. A 413 wedge V-8 called the Ram Charger was offered, but mainly for drag race competition, in the Dodge.

Studebaker, after its 1959 spurt, was faltering again even though the restyled Hawk of 1962 was a beautiful car. In an effort to increase its flagging market penetration, Studebaker came out with the stunning Avanti. Raymond Loewy was responsible for the Avanti's design which was unlike anything else on the road. It had a coke bottle profile and upswept rear. At the front two large square bezels housed the single headlights and a large air scoop was tucked beneath the slender bumper. There was no grille. That it was aerodynamic was shortly borne out when it grabbed every USAC record and tore across Bonneville at 170.78 mph for the flying mile.

The car was manufactured out of fiberglass but early production difficulties were responsible for large numbers of advance order customers giving up and buying the new Corvette Stingray instead. Only 4600 Avantis finally left the factory by the time Studebaker called it quits at the end of '63 and moved to

Hamilton, Ontario, where Canadian Larks continued until the final end in 1966.

The year 1963 gave birth to the best looking Buick ever built. This was the luxury personal Riviera Sports Coupe designed to halt the runaway success of the Thunderbird. William L. Mitchell, then head of GM styling (he replaced Harley Earl), was the man behind the crisp, razor edged lines inspired, perhaps, by European influences. Everything about the Riviera looked right and was unlike anything else in Buicks prodigious and varied model line-up. With the exception of air conditioning, a $350 extra, almost everything was standard for a giveaway $4333. The car met with public approval and some 40,000 were sold.

For new and specialised models 1963 was GM's year all the way. Besides the Riviera there was the new Corvette Sting Ray and Pontiac put out a sleek, re-styled Grand Prix, another contender for Thunderbird's crown. After three years with its cigar-shaped profile, the T-Bird would be all new for 1964.

Ever since its debut, the Corvette had followed a policy of continuous improvement. It had remained with the same body since 1956, concentrating more on what went on underneath the attractive fiberglass shell. In 1963 Chevrolet changed everything and the new Corvette Sting Ray was a vast improvement over the old. In fact the only carry-over from 1962 were the engines – they were so good they didn't need improvement.

The new shape had its beginnings in the Bill Mitchell designed Sting Ray prototype and earlier racing car project. The production Sting Ray had elements of these designs in its own and the overall effect was stunning. On the coupe the doors cut into the roof, though not as much as the famous gullwing Mercedes, and the front and rear fenders had a pronounced hump over the wheel arches. From the rear, the fastback coupe gave the impression of a jet liner's forward section. The Mitchell designed rear split window added to the illusion.

Chassis, engines and suspensions were the province of Zora Arkus Duntov and had been since 1956. The Sting Ray was given full independent suspension, quicker steering and an aluminium clutch housing. Apparently over 85% of the buyers ordered a manual gearbox with their Corvette, the majority plumping for the four-speed unit. Biggest engine was the 327 rated at 360 hp with fuel injection, the smallest, 250 hp.

From 1963 to 1967 116,964 Sting Rays were produced, far more than during the previous 10 years. Even better was the '68–'72 period when over 130,000 were built with the later body, which stayed in production for 15 years. Stand up there, the man who said Detroit practises planned obsolescence!!

The AMA's 1957 ban on manufacturer participation in motor sport was fraying at the edges by the early 'sixties and just seemed to fade away. Car makers were openly flaunting the ruling and becoming more and more involved in racing. Then Ford dropped the cat among the pigeons – henceforth the company would be following a policy of Total Performance. From 1964 until the end of the decade, there would appear on the streets of America, some of the wildest cars ever to come out of a factory, anywhere in the world. It was total war…

Le Mans 1966, a gray Sunday afternoon in June. The 24-hour classic was only seconds away from its finish. Then they appeared, victorious but graceful as they crossed the finish line, one, two, three. A surge of patriotic sentiment welled in the hearts of Americans everywhere. Ford GT-40s had brought home to America the world's most coveted racing honor and they had done it in style. One, two, three; if nothing else, it made the millions spent on Total Performance all worthwhile.

The Shelby and Holman & Moody built GT-40s repeated their triumph in 1967, becoming the first marque ever to win Le Mans two years in a row. Ford, satisfied with its tremendous success, withdrew its support but a Gulf Oil sponsored GT-40 won again in 1969. These and other major international wins were fitting reward for the long hours and sleepless nights that went into designing, building and testing the cars. It was an amazing achievement, all the more so considering it took just a little over two years from design board to the winning cars.

During 1963 Ford started racing with a vengeance on the NASCAR circuits. A handsome 23 races were won in big Galaxie 500s with 425 horses under their hoods. In the Super/Stock class, Plymouth and Dodge had it all their own way and there would be trouble in the '64 season with new generation, hemi powered cars from Chrysler's stable.

Those who benefit most from factory competition are the buying public. Racing activity shows up weaknesses and the strength of the cars and any improvements made are handed on to the customer. The

manufacturers themselves also do well out of racing through advertising, publicity for a particular make and increased sales of its lesser kindred.

Ever since Bunkie Knudsen transformed Pontiac's image into a performance car, it had been winning races (22 NASCAR wins out of 53 in 1962). For the 1963 racing program Pontiac engineers were working on lighter cars to wrap round their potent 421 engine. Lighter meant many aluminium parts but GM's hierarchy, conservative to the point of square, heard what was going on and promptly banned both Pontiac and Chevrolet from any more racing activities. So the divisions concentrated on high powered street cars with an eye on future competitive involvement.

The Tempest/Le Mans compact became an intermediate when it was given a new and longer body in 1964. It was a good car so Pontiac decided to make it even better. This was accomplished with a 389 c.i.d. engine, heavy duty suspension and a four-speed manual transmission. Finally it was given a European flavor – perhaps Ferrari flavor might be more accurate – and christened GTO.

A lot of the credit for Pontiac's GTO and later excellent cars, belongs to livewire, but tarnished genius, John DeLorean. He had been with Pontiac for nine years, becoming general manager in 1965. He was responsible for turning the Grand Prix from a woolly car into a taut, GT type automobile. DeLorean was much involved in the development of Pontiac's advanced OHC six cylinder engine and the division's belated answer to Ford's Mustang, the Firebird. A good idea of DeLorean's success can be found in Pontiac's sales figures; in 1956; when he joined the division produced 405,730 units compared with 910,977 in 1968, a year before he moved over to Chevrolet.

There were fears heads would roll if the new GTO was marketed as a separate model due to corporate heads' dislike for anything smacking of performance. So the '64 and '65 models were sold as a Le Mans option. Sales were phenomenal and the brass, who like money, sanctioned the car as a separate series from 1966.

The initial GTO was a great car made even better as the years rolled on. It had a lot to answer for as it is regarded as the father of the whole muscle/pony-car movement which slipped into high gear at the end of 1964 when Ford's legendary Mustang galloped on to the scene.

Lido A. Iacocca, better known as Lee, succeeded as Ford division's general manager after Robert McNamara became company president. Genial and outgoing, but a skilful operator with a finger very much on the market's pulse, Iacocca headed the team responsible for the Mustang. It was to appeal to the youth market, have bucket seats, choice of engines and transmissions and apart from the stylish, sporty looking body, the Mustang would use existing Falcon and Fairlane parts.

Although billed as a 1965 model, the Mustang was unveiled to the public on April 17th 1964. Offered as a convertible, hardtop and two plus two fastback, the sleek little car with the high placed grille was a success beyond Ford's wildest dreams. Between April 1964 and December 1965, 680,989 units were built. Best sellers were the hardtops equipped with the 289 cubic inch V-8 in various stages of tune but the base engine was Ford's reliable 170 c.i.d. six with about as much go as a three-legged tortoise.

While the Mustang was making headlines, Plymouth wasn't exactly idle. About the time Mustang made its appearance Plymouth announced a sporty variation of its popular Valiant compact. Sporting a fastback body, a slightly different grille and the biggest rear window to be found on any car, it dispensed with animal names favoring that of a fish instead: the Barracuda. Standard engine was the 170 c.i.d. six but Chrysler's new 273 c.i.d. V-8, coupled with a four-speed manual transmission, gave the Barracuda pretty good performance.

As if to emphasise the importance of Total Performance, Ford entered a team of well prepared Falcons in the gruelling Monte Carlo Rally. Crysler was represented too, with three V-8 powered Valiants, whose 1963 restyling followed traditional lines. This was Valiant's first Monte Carlo outing, Falcon's second and the experience told. Falcon took 2nd overall, a 1st and 2nd in its class and fastest time over five of the six special stages. Eight Falcons had entered and eight finished. Of the Valiants, one failed to finish but the others came in 88th and 146th overall.

Averaging 105 mph over 100,000 miles at Daytona International Speedway, Mercury Comet's incredible durability feat helped sales and inspired a racy two door hardtop called the Cyclone. Equipped with the 225 hp 289 V-8, Motor Trend's test Cyclone took 8.8 secs. to reach 60 mph, not bad for a car weighing 3060 lbs and a clear indication that the optional 271 hp version was a real barnstormer. In the same issue the magazine tested a fastback Mustang GT 350. This was the first of the famous Cobra Mustangs and the test-car clocked a zero to 60 time in 7.0 secs. It used the 289 but the big difference between it and other 289s was that this one had been rebuilt by Carroll Shelby who tweaked it to 306 hp.

Carroll Shelby is one of the all-time greats in the racing world and builder of the venomous Cobra 427, a sportscar that blew the likes of Ferrari clear into the weeds. The Cobra story began in 1962 when Shelby reached an agreement with AC Cars of Thames Ditton, England, to put prepared Ford 289s into AC bodies. In this guise, the AC Cobras dominated SCCA competition, and full order books were a foregone conclusion.

The AC Cobras were still being put together at Shelby's Venice workshop outside Los Angeles, when Ford approached him to make something of the Mustang and to handle the company's racing operations (it was Shelby who built the Le Mans winning GT-40). The 1965 fastback was the first of a long line of Mustangs to be given Shelby's magic.

The mid-sixties could be classed as Detroit's finest post-war period if only for the bewildering choice of models and different breeds of cars facing the buyer. The big luxury sedans, like Buick's Electra 225 or the Chrysler New Yorker Salon, came with almost every single accessory you care to name, as standard equipment (in the Chrysler's case, the only options were full leather interior, limited slip differential and tilt steering) at what now seems like a giveaway price of around $6500. Further up the scale, Continental, Cadillac and Imperial might nudge $7800. At the low end, Chevrolet, Ford and Plymouth had option lists as long as your arm and there was a time when Chevrolet could boast that no two cars were alike. Then came the economic compacts, the sporty compacts, the powder puff intermediates like Oldsmobile's Cutlass Holiday Coupe and then the out and out brute force cars with acres of go but little space to stop – some of the earlier muscle cars had a disconcerting habit of running out of brakes at the most inappropriate times.

As the cars got faster, racing experience began to show. Brakes, rarely a good point on American cars, improved dramatically when the manufacturers decided discs were a better bet than drums. Thunderbird and Corvette were first to offer them, soon to be followed by everyone else. Now the cars could stop as well as go. Technology, which had brought the Corvair, an aluminium V-8 and the '63 Corvette, got another boost the day Oldsmobile announced its front wheel drive Toronado.

As far as Motor Trend was concerned it was no contest when it came to handing out its Car of the Year award. "... never in the 14-year history of this award has the choice been so obvious and unanimous", enthused the editor. And he was right. The Toronado was the first front wheel drive car since the 1936 Cord and it was also the biggest. Top Oldsmobile men like Chief Engineer John Beltz, Advanced Design Engineer A. K. Watt, Asst. Chief Designer David R. North (the Toronado was based upon his idea of the kind of car he'd like to own) and Vice-President of Styling, Bill Mitchell who okayed the design, these and other distinguished talents were involved in bringing the Toronado to life. That they managed to perfect a "fwd" system strong enough to handle a 425 c.i.d. V-8, in a car 211 inches long, is nothing short of miraculous. The Toronado could out-handle any other car its size, and with speeds well in excess of 125 mph, could outrun most.

A sculptured ledge ran the full length of the Toronado's profile as part of the dramatically flared wheel arches. The sharply defined front fenders fared into the elegant bumper assembly and the long hood dipped to meet the narrow, full width simple grille. Inboard retractable dual headlights fitted snugly into recesses above the grille and were electrically operated. The beautifully styled roof flowed in an unbroken line to the rear bumper and the overall effect was as aesthetically pleasing as a Renoir. There was no other car like it: the restyled Riviera shared the same body shell but looked nothing like the Toronado. Oldsmobile's "fwd" car was on its own – number one in a field of one.

Elwood Engle's styling influence manifested itself on the 1965 Chrysler line. Actually, his first design was the 1964 Imperial. Certainly the best looking since 1957, the Imperial, and the later Chryslers, owed a lot to Engle's Continental, which was hardly surprising. 1965 was the last year for the 300 Letter Series, by now little more than a luxury version of the standard 300. The race winning hemi was released for street use in 1966, much to the delight of the speed set.

Ralph Nader was the motor industry's bad dream through the 'sixties. His book, "Unsafe at any Speed", was an unwarranted, ill-researched attack on the Corvair, claiming anyone buying a Corvair was signing his death certificate, due to the car's alleged tendency to flip over onto its roof. True, the early Corvair's suspension was a bit basic but was corrected in 1962. Major improvements occurred in the redesigned 1965 models transforming the Corvair into a delightful, good handling car. The widely held belief that Nader's book was responsible for Corvair's 1969 demise, is incorrect. GM doesn't like losers

and the Corvair's fate was sealed by management several months before the book came out. The car didn't come up to expectations in the sales battle with Ford's Falcon and that was that.

Nader's book had repercussions for the industry as a whole, however. The high annual carnage on America's highways forced Congress to pass safety legislation taking effect from 1967. Another bill called for strict exhaust emission controls to cut down the amount of lead and carbons polluting the air. To meet these requirements effectively meant the end of the all-powerful muscle car.

But it wasn't dead yet and still had a few years to go. By 1967 the muscle car had become a powerful sales force. And to make the most of a good thing, the manufacturers happily obliged. Even luxury cars didn't escape; 7 liter engines turned up in Chevrolet's full-size Caprice and Ford's LTD with blistering acceleration to match. Talking of acceleration, 390 c.i.d. equipped Mustangs were coming off the line in 7½ seconds; even quicker was Buick's GS 400 turning in 0-60 times of six seconds flat.

Cadillac made big news in 1967 with its "fwd" Eldorado. It had its own engine and differed a little in its approach to fwd from the Toronado on which it was based. Its sleek, razor edge styling gave the Eldorado a vaguely teutonic air but it was the best-looking Cadillac since 1940. Over the years the Eldorado, Toronado and Riviera have become world leaders in terms of innovative technology, form and function.

American Motors hadn't ignored the muscle car boom even though the company was better known for its economical, well built smaller cars. 428,346 cars left AMC's factory in 1963, the year Rambler was chosen as Motor Trend's Car of the Year. A half-hearted attempt at a sporty image was tried with the 1965 Rambler Marlin, a fastback similar to the Barracuda. Hastily contrived, the Marlin took 12 seconds and more to reach 60 mph from zero. Renamed the AMC Marlin in 1966, it was given a 280 hp engine which quickened its pace. The public didn't like it and the Marlin was dropped after 1967.

Much better was the Rogue. Based on the faithful American compact, the Rogue had a 390 c.i.d. V-8 rated at 315 hp. At the same time the Rebel SST, a hotted-up Rambler, was introduced. Neither had the performance offered by the Big Three muscle cars and consequently, didn't sell as well, either.

AMC had its Mustang chasers as well. Both the Mustang sized Javelin and AMX appeared in 1968. Both were attractive looking cars, the AMX especially so. It was a truncated version of the Javelin with a section chopped out of the middle to create a two-seater. Richard Teague, AMC's chief stylist, takes the credit for a superb design. The AMX handled well and went even better with the 390 under the hood; 0-60 in 6.9 seconds put it up with the heavyweights. The Javelin, too, could have the 390 (this engine was an option on both cars) which made it a real stormer.

The wildly successful Mustang was lengthened and given a mild facelift for 1967. With the 390 rated at 335 hp, Ford's ponycar was a mean machine. Even meaner was the Shelby 350 Cobra Mustang. Shelby was sent basic cars which were reworked with goodies like Koni shocks, traction bars, fiberglass hood and the 289 was rebuilt to give 306 hp. More power came from the GT 500 Mustang equipped with the 428 engine. It delivered shattering performance for a mere $4195.

Belated but well worth the wait, were GM's ponycars. Announced simultaneously, Chevrolet's Camaro and the Pontiac Firebird shared the same unit body and front sub-frame but developed their own distinct personalities. Designed by the great Bill Mitchell and his talented team, both cars had beautiful shapes based upon the fashionable coke bottle styling resulting in an overall effect which was cleaner, more cohesive than their rivals.

Standard engines were sixes; an OHV for Camaro; two versions of Pontiac's OHC for the Firebird. V-8 options – the ones most folk bought – climbed all the way to 400 cubic inches. Of particular interest was the Camaro X-28 model. This was a real high performance car originally built for the SCCA Trans-Am. racing events. Prepared Z-28s came third in the 1967 Championship, first and second in its class in 1968 and 1969. A special Firebird derivative, the legendary Trans-Am, first appeared in 1969.

On the intermediate muscle car front Pontiac still had its GTO. Restyled in 1966 the GTO could turn in zero to 60 between 6.2 and 6.6 seconds by 1967, if it had the 400 c.i.d. engine. In fact, most of the supercars could come off the line faster than that.

SS396, Z-28, AMX, GTO, GTA, GS400, SST, there seemed no end to letter and numeral combinations the manufacturers used to describe their supercars. Ford was more inclined to use names, one such being the Torino. In top form the Torino was mated to the 427 rated at 390 hp. Its fastback design made the car eminently suitable for the NASCAR ovals and it took 20 firsts during the 1968 season.

Chrysler wasn't standing still watching its competitors' antics; in fact Chrysler's supercars were the ones that made GM and Ford nervous. Especially in 1968 when Dodge launched its Scatpack campaign while Plymouth was "out to win you over". The line-up was extensive; almost every model in Dodge and Plymouth camps could be had as a musclecar and that didn't include the ones specially made for the task.

A completely new Dodge Charger was launched for 1968. It was easily the best looking supercar around. Standing still it looked like a speeding bullet, an effect achieved by softening the coke bottle line. A recessed rear window nestled between is wide, but sharply raked, C-pillars. Many of you will know the car; it was the one the baddies drove in "Bullitt", and the "Dukes of Hazzard" General Lee is a 1970 Charger R/T. Top engines were either the 440 c.i.d. wedge or the awesome 426 hemi. In R/T form, a Charger recorded 0-60 times in 4.2 to 4.9 seconds depending on which magazine you read.

Dodge also had the Charger Super Bee "with the bumble bee stripes". These were racing type decals wrapped round the car's rear and part of the Scat Pack which had a cartoon bee as its trademark. Another part of the Scat Pack was the pretty two door Dart GTS, a hotted-up version of Dodge's popular compact. Sister division Plymouth fielded a stylish Barracuda which was given a new shape in 1967. It looked a little like the Charger's small brother but had a flowing, notchback roof and deeply recessed twin grilles.

Belvedere used to be Plymouth's full-size model but that became the Fury. Demotion followed and the name was given to an intermediate series. By 1968, the Belvedere had spawned a host of siblings; the Satellite, Road Runner and GTX. The Satellite was more luxurious than the Road Runner, the latter a unique combination of power and austerity. The name came from the Warner Bros. cartoon character and the car had Road Runner decals stuck on the sides of the rear fenders.

The idea of the Road Runner was to give performance wrapped in a plain package to keep the price under $3000. It succeeded handsomely, was loved by press and public alike and sold in large numbers. The car was characterised by a horn which went "beep-beep" like the cartoon bird. One area in which Dodge and Plymouth scored over their rivals, was in handling. In the case of the Road Runner, it was better than its own kind and possibly the fastest. Even with the 383 c.i.d. it only took five seconds to reach 60; the mind boggles at what it could do with either the 440 or 426 hemi.

The GTX was described as a "bomb" by one automotive magazine who turned in a quarter-mile time of 13.43 secs. at a terminal speed of 96 mph. This was with the hemi engine which enabled the car to reach 145 mph in stock, showroom trim. Handling was good but not *that* good due to the top heavy front end plus drastic understeer. As a straight line traffic-light stormer, the GTX could hardly be beaten.

GTO, the granddaddy of the supercar boom, restyled for 1968, bore a family resemblance to the Firebird. It was also just as quick if it had the 400 engine. A variation of the GTO was the Judge, distinguished by colorful decals of its name at strategic points on the body. Although the car looked impressive – it had a front spoiler and horizontal wing bolted to the trunk – its handling wasn't a patch on the regular GTO. Enthusiasts left it alone, considering it a car for those who preferred flash to dash.

Emission and safety regulations were getting tougher all the while and insurance companies, who looked upon muscle with alarm, were charging premiums so high that prospective owners were either put off or took out a second mortgage! The great days of the musclecar were numbered and in some ways the industry itself was to blame. It could be said, with reasonable justification, that they killed the goose that laid the golden egg through over-production, too many models and too much emphasis on brute power. Had they concentrated on fewer models and on making them truly roadworthy, as they do today, things might have been different.

The high point of the musclecar was reached during 1969 and 1970. Dodge and Plymouth, although they were winning races at NASCAR, weren't winning enough. A more than satisfactory solution was found in the Dodge Daytona 500 (1969) and Plymouth Superbird (1970). There has never been anything like these two, before or since.

Both cars used the Coronet/Belvedere body but to make them more aerodynamic Dodge and Plymouth tacked on a long, sloping pointed nose, flush mounted the rear window and installed a huge, strut-mounted airfoil – not unlike the tail of a Boeing 727. Both cars had either the hemi or 440 engine and in this form the Winged Warriors, as they were nicknamed, won 38 out of 48 races in the NASCAR Championships during the 1970 season. To enable them to race, they had to qualify as production cars so Dodge built 500 Daytonas, Plymouth 1920 Superbirds. Because they were designed for competition the Superbird and Daytona were the nearest thing to a true racing car that could be bought off the showroom floor. Scarcity of numbers make them highly desirable and they fetch a premium price today.

At the end of the 'sixties even the luxury and standard cars had whopping big engines. The Eldorado boasted 472 cubic inches and its major rival, the Continental Mark III, had 460. This new addition to the Continental saga, introduced for 1968, had the longest hood of any car at the time – six feet of it! It was an attractive car with concealed headlights and a Rolls-cum-Mercedes upright grille. It had every option known to man, many as standard fittings and sold almost as many units as the Eldorado.

1970 and a new decade. A decade which would bring profound changes to an industry raised on horsepower and gloss. Federal regulations, politicians and the 1973 oil embargo put paid to the musclecars and as the 'seventies wore on, big cars were regarded as a wasteful extravaganza. Detroit went through a crisis period, not sure which way to turn, what to do. Their first small cars were poor, badly made substitutes for the European and Japanese models that were selling so well. By the 'eighties, Detroit got its act together and the cars produced today are a match for those of Japan and Europe.

America's motor industry is the greatest in the world. It is versatile, colorful and ingenious. Where else would you find the flamboyance of the 'fifties, the excitement of the 'sixties? It, the motorcar, is as much a part of America's heritage as Abraham Lincoln. That's something not even the Japanese can take away.

Automotive writers' reaction was guarded when they reviewed the first Mustangs to go on sale. They had hoped for something closer to Ford's showcar, also called Mustang, which had four wheel independent suspension and a centrally located engine with a transaxle unit. What the world got, at Ford division's general manager Lee Iacocca's behest, was a sporty type car cobbled up from Falcon and Fairlane bits. The logic was to keep costs down and market it around $2500; a price most people could afford.

It's no use dreaming of Mercedes-Benz technology in a $2500 car no matter what the pundits think. The general public liked what it saw and bought over half a million Mustangs in the marque's first year. Part of its success was the seemingly endless option list allowing the customer to virtually create his own car. The base Mustang came with a six cylinder engine but most people selected one of the three V-8s available. Three or four speed manual and automatic transmissions, handling packages and vanity options could turn the Mustang into a powder puff or a solid performance car.

1966 was Mustang's second year and sales went up to over 600,000. Best selling model was the hardtop equipped with the 289 cu. in. V-8. Over 56,000 convertibles were built, like the '66 model shown. Note: the engine is the 289. The chrome pony, set in the recessed grille, coined the name used to describe a host of similar . . . ponycars! The standard buckets were quite comfortable and instruments reasonably legible. Lindsey Goodman, Auburn, Ind., owner.

The Sedanet or Fastback styling theme had been used by Buick since 1941 and nowhere was it more attractive than on the 1949 Roadmaster Sedanet Model 76-S. New were the "portholes" on the front fenders, a styling gimmick that has remained a Buick trademark to this day. Note the massive over-riders on the front bumper; this was an optional feature probably designed for aggressive parking! This car belongs to the A-C-D Museum, Auburn, Ind.

At the top of the post-World War II range was the Fleetwood 75, or luxury for nine. And if a regular Cadillac seemed big, this one's vital statistics were formidable: a wheelbase just short of 150 inches, a bumper to bumper length of 236 inches and a dry weight well over 5,000 pounds. Four cigar lighters, two electric clocks, and power brakes, seats, windows and divider were part of this 1956 package; air conditioning was an established regular option. Paintwork was usually black, although interior fabrics came in a pretty wide choice of broadcloths or Bedford Cords. Demand was limited but steady at 1,500-2,000 units a year during the 50s. The 75 wasn't, of course, the largest Cadillac: one step further still was the Professional Car Chassis for ambulance and hearse bodies which ran to 158 inches of wheelbase in 1956.

1957's super-car; the Eldorado Brougham with air suspension, cost $13,074, as against $6,648 for the exotic Eldorado Biarritz convertible, and a mere $4,713 for a 62 sedan. Styling was four-door pillarless hardtop *below* and the brushed stainless steel top shows up well in these pictures. Detail was most elaborate, as witness the smoker's companion *top right* and the big glovebox on the facia *top left* which came complete with six magnetised tumblers, cigarette case, lipstick, and stick cologne.

Gasoline was still cheap, congestion problems as yet unfaced, and seat belts confined to the catalog's small print when this 1959 Cadillac 62 convertible was built, one of an impressive 11,130 to leave the factory that year. Total model-year production was 142,272 units. With only a single quadrajet carburettor on this version of the 390 ci motor, output was down to 320 horsepower. A full length side rubbing strip is the easiest way to tell the cheaper ragtop from the Biarritz.

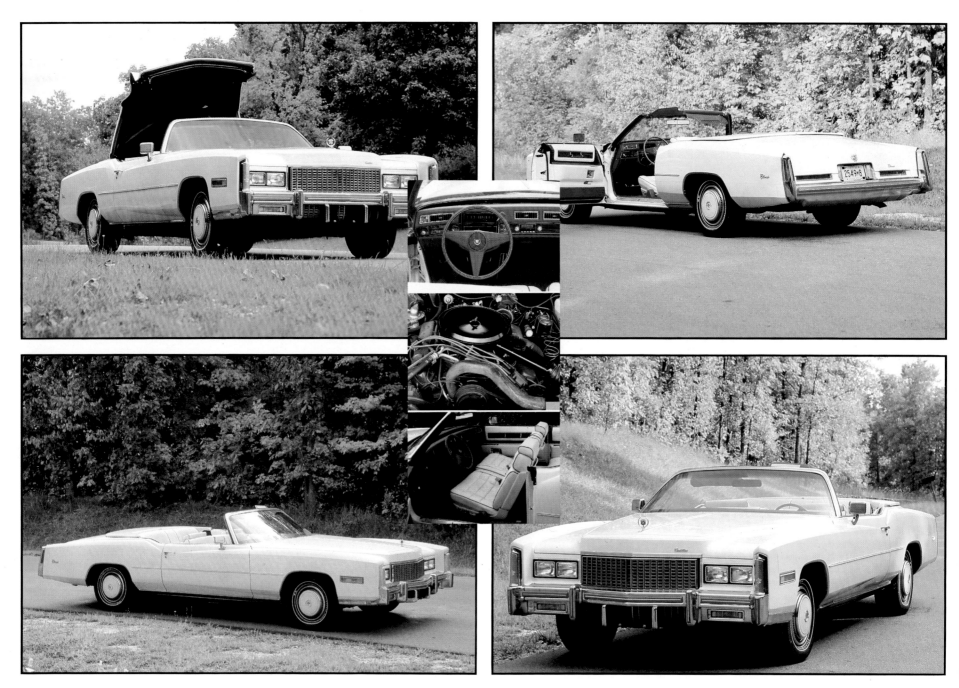

1966 saw the last of the Eldorado convertibles and the last of the giant engines, since Cadillac went down to 425 ci in 1977. This car had four-wheel disc brakes and was available with electronic fuel injection. Shown is one of 200 'limited edition' white cars which marked (or so they thought) the end of the ragtop era. Cadillac had, however, already delivered another 13,800 standard cars before this publicity gesture. List price was $11,049, but in that summer's brief auction boom new examples were changing hands for over twenty grand.

The breathtaking 1963 Riviera Sport Coupe was Buick's entry into the Thunderbird dominated "personal luxury" car market. Its razor-edged design was unlike anything else produced by GM, possessing an elegance and poise that set it apart from the rest. The Riviera was pure artistry on wheels, thanks to the gifted William L. Mitchell who blended a subtle mix of European and American influences to create a true classic. This example belongs to Larry K. Riesen, Fort Wayne, Ind.

The finest of wood and steel crafted automobiles, the Chrysler Town & Country was arguably the original personal luxury car; the toy of the Hollywood highflyers. This mint 1948 example belongs to T & C buff, Roy Bleeke of Fort Wayne, and shows how well the handcrafted wood sections blend into the body. Huge overriders set off the heavily chromed grille, behind which nestles Chrysler's C-39 Spitfire Straight Eight rated at 135 hp. The Town & Country came with most options as standard, including Chrysler's semi-automatic Fluid Drive transmission and leather upholstery. Total cost in 1948 was $3420. A cheaper version, a four door sedan on a shorter wheelbase, was also available.

Wayne E. Boyd of Auburn, Ind. is the owner of this immaculate 1966 Chrysler 300 convertible *left*. Not to be confused with the GT type letter series 300, the pretender replaced the Windsor model and adopted the 300 nomenclature in the hope that its reputation would help sales. The standard engine was a 383 rated at 315 hp.

1955 thru 1957 Chevrolets are much sought after by collectors, today. One highly prized model is the attractively designed Nomad station wagon which is conservatively valued at anything between $12,000-$15,000 – new it cost $2,571. Although much the same as regular Chevies, it was its distinctive roof design that set it apart. The photographs *above* illustrate the differences, including the sloped back pillar and large glass area, very well. This example is the 1957 model belonging to Rick Carroll of Jensen Beach, Fla.

① ② ③ ④

Chevrolet produced 1,713,478 units for model year 1955; 773,238 of them Bel Airs (1). All new styling and the first Chevrolet V-8 engine since 1917 made it popular then and a collector's item now. The new engine displaced 265 cubic inches and developed 162 hp combined with the three speed manual transmission, or 170 hp hooked up to the automatic 2 speed Powerglide unit. Mike Triboulet owns this one and Nelson Bandy the 1956 model (2,4,& 5), a two door Bel Air Sedan. Minor trim detailing and a full width grille were the only differences between the 1955 and 1956 models and 1,574,740 of the latter were produced – 138,738 down on the previous year.

Kevin E. Dooley's 1964 Corvair Monza Spyder convertible was in its last year with the original body style (3) and 1965 would see a new and much improved Corvair. The Monza Spyder was a sporty model introduced in 1962. Its air cooled rear mounted flat six engine developed 80 hp in regular versions but Spyder models had a 150 hp turbo-charged unit.

Chevrolet's Camaro arrived on the motoring scene a little more than two years after Ford's successful Mustang. Launched at the same time as near identical twin, Pontiac's Firebird, Chevrolet initially dished up the impressive Z/28 option for racing use. In this guise, the Camaro beat factory backed Mustangs in the last two races of the 1967 Trans-Am season followed by a first and second in the Trans-Am class in the 12 hour 1968 Sebring event. The 1969 Z-28 shown here, has the small block 302 cid V-8. 0 – 60 with the 302 was slightly over 7 seconds but the standing quarter, according to road tests, was a phenomenal 14.85 at 101.4 mph. This example belongs to the A-C-D Museum, Auburn, Ind.

The Billie Joe Spears song, "'57 Chevrolet" is a loving tribute to one of the best Chevrolets ever made. Its durability can be attested to by its extraordinarily high survival rate. An option on the '57s was the famous 283 cid V-8 rated at 283 hp, or one horsepower per cubic inch. Robert Rodgers is the car's proud owner.

Bill Mitchell designed it, Zora Arkus Duntov engineered it and the result was the 1963 Corvette Stingray shown here. The semi-boat tail rear, novel split rear window design and pivoting, hidden headlights caused a sensation in motoring circles throughout the world. With its all round independent suspension, choice of engines and fuel injection, the fiberglass bodied Stingray was a match for most European sportscars, even more so with the addition of four wheel disc brakes in 1965. Offered as a coupe and convertible, the Stingray met with immediate public acceptance to the tune of 21,000 produced, some 7000 up on the previous model.

Auburn, Ind. dentist Mike Hayes, spotted this Stingray for sale at a Kruse auction. The car didn't sell, fortunately for Mr. Hayes, who haggled a price and became the Stingray's new owner.

Chrome plate and stainless trim were in abundance on GM's 1958 models, the new Chevrolet Bel Air Impala Sport Coupe being no exception. New from the ground up, the Chevrolet had a 117.5 inch wheelbase and a length of 209 inches compared to the '57's 115 and 200 inches. Interiors were attractive in an extrovert sort of way and the steering wheel was supposed to remind you that perhaps a Corvette was in your future. Owned by Mike Triboulet.

Radio manufacturer Powell Crosley went into the economy car business in 1939. After the war Crosleys sold quite well but innovations like four wheel disc brakes and stamped sheet metal four cylinder engines suffered numerous problems. 1952 was the last year of the Crosley, now with drum brakes and a cast iron four ... unfortunately nobody wanted econocars in the days when everything big was better. This 1952 car is owned by John E. Nichols, Fla.

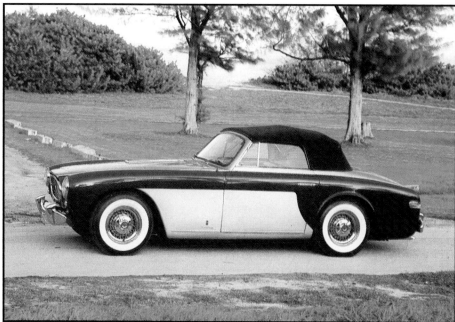

Losing $50,000 a year for five years pursuing a dream hurts even wealthy men like Briggs Cunningham. That's what it cost him in his attempt to win Le Mans with an all American car. He came very close to achieving his aim with a third place in his Chrysler hemi powered Cunningham C-5R.

Much later, Cunningham was to say that if he had been supplied with the disc brakes he wanted, his cars would have won at Le Mans. There's no reason to doubt his word; after all, in the 1953 race the C-5R was timed at 156 mph and the Cunninghams had the stamina to finish the gruelling 24 hour event while many European racers failed.

The car pictured here is not one of the racing Cunninghams but the 1953 C-3 "production" model. Styled by Michelotti, then working for Vignale, the Italian coachbuilders, the C-3 was one of only two 1953 American cars to be included in the New York Museum of Modern Art's list of the world's Ten Best Cars. Looking at the picture of the car taken on a late Fall evening in Florida, courtesy of the Elliott Museum at Stuart, it's not hard to see why it was picked. Under the hood is the all-powerful Chrysler hemi which turns this sleek grand tourer into a potent piece of transportation.

A glance at this car, with its continental spare wheel cover, wire wheels and narrow windshield, tells you it must be the ultra expensive 1953 Skylark, built to celebrate Buick's 50th Anniversary.

The Skylark came with every option as standard equipment and cost $4600. The high price put off a lot of buyers and only 1690 units were built. Buick tried again with a smaller version in 1954 and a price reduction of $300. This one only sold 836 units and it was dropped at the end of the year. Of the two versions, the '53 was a far better looking automobile with a level of quality workmanship sadly lacking in today's cars. Although the skylark shared its toothy grin with lesser Buicks, its lines were reasonably free of embellishments and was notable for its lack of "portholes." Ron Lintz is the owner.

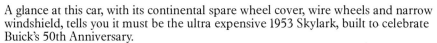

Not everything that came out of Detroit during the fifties was trimmed to excess. In fact the "creme de la creme" of Chrysler's 1955 crop, the C-300, had extremely clean lines. This beautiful car, styled by Virgil Exner, had a New Yorker body and an Imperial grille but the effect was striking.

The C-300 was a true grand tourer in every sense of the description. It was also the hottest car produced by a U.S. manufacturer, a point soon realised by drivers of rival makes competing in the NASCAR, AAA and Daytona Speedweeks championships. The big, white 300 horsepower chargers won almost everything in sight and became the first and only car to win all three championships at once, thanks to sponsor Carl Kiekhaufer of Mercury Outboard Motors. Our pictures show singer Richard Carpenter's pristine example.

Two years after Chrysler Corporation's "Suddenly it's 1960" look, Virgil Exner's finny styling was beginning to pall with the addition of hastily contrived trim and disorientated grilles, as in the case of this 1959 De Soto FireFlite convertible. This was unfortunate because De Soto was a fine handling automobile with power to match. More unfortunate was De Soto's position, sandwiched between the popular Dodge and Chrysler models. Dodge went upmarket and nibbled away De Soto sales while Chrysler tore at the upper end of the market.

A styling feature since 1956 were De Soto's taillights. Attractive they were; but vulnerable to parking lot benders. Poor sales drove De Soto to extinction in 1961. Car shown belongs to Gerald Paradise.

The $250 million certainty that failed is one way of describing the luckless Edsel. Launched in 1958 to bolster Ford's mid-price range, the Edsel was supposed to take away sales from GM and Chrysler's medium price cars. Nearly ten years of research went into the Edsel and included an intense market survey, the results of which augured well for a new mid-priced automobile. Sadly, the market research people were way off course.

A publicity campaign designed to whet consumers' appetites was the only thing to succeed about the Edsel. It gave the impression that the Edsel was radically different from anything that had gone before. So it was with great disappointment that prospective customers viewed the Edsel for the first time. It was utterly conventional save the vertical "horse-collar" grille and automatic shift buttons set in the steering wheel hub.

The Edsel couldn't have been launched at a worse time. 1958 was the Eisenhower recession year and medium-price car sales slumped alarmingly. Three years later the Edsel was no more.

The pictures show the slightly cleaned up 1959 Ranger model equipped with the 303 bhp V-8. The car belongs to Denis Winebrenner, Auburn, Ind.

It looked like a car, it rode like a car but there the similarity ended. In 1957 Ford announced a new vehicle; the Ranchero half-ton pickup. Pickups had been around for a long time but they looked like small trucks. The Ranchero combined the best of both worlds providing utility with style. The beautiful red and white example above, belongs to Bill Arnold of Petersburg, Ind., and has Ford's 223 cu. in. Mileage Maker Six under the hood.

If ever there was a car that epitomised the flamboyant fifties then Ford's Skyliner Retractable Hardtop has to be a strong contender for the crown. This extraordinary Ford, with an aircraft carrier deck, had to be seen to be believed.

The retractable steel top was originally meant for the 1956 Continental Mk. II. After 2.2 million had been spent on the top, planners deemed it too costly for the already expensive limited edition Mk. II. So Ford got it, spent a further $18 million and lo! the Skyliner Retractable made its debut in 1957. First year sales of 20,766 hardtop convertibles appeared to justify designer Gilbert Spear's concept and were only a few hundred less than the Thunderbird.

The roof mechanism consisted of five motors, 13 switches, 10 solenoids, nine circuit breakers and 610 feet of wiring. When the "retract" switch is moved, the front section of the roof folds under and the top gracefully begins its descent into the oversize trunk. Oversize the trunk may have been but with the top down there was hardly room for a toothbrush! Delbert Fellers has owned his torch red example from new since 1959; the Skyliner's last year of production – a fabulous bit of nonsense that made living worthwhile.

As the cheerful but gimmicky Skyliner faded into the sunset of the fifties, it ushered in new, conservative thinking in the form of the compact Falcon. This was Ford's contender in the small car stakes and was pitted against GM's Corvair, Chrysler's Valiant, American Motors' Rambler American and Studebaker's Lark. Powered by a thrifty 170 cu. in. six, the entirely conventional Falcon rode well, stopped well, was tough and outsold the opposition all down the line. The 1962 model shown differs only slightly from the 1960 version. A convex grille, new bumper and phoney hood scoop are the only alterations. The big, round taillights were a Ford trademark for a number of years and the rubbing strip along the sides is an aftermarket accessory.

This is a Ford that meant business, a car not to be treated lightly. A very special Mustang because it is a Shelby Cobra Mustang GT 500.

From the beginning, Ford handed Carroll Shelby Mustangs to perform his magic and turn them into stiff handling, gut churning automobiles. Ford, very much into its Total Performance kick, considered Shelby Mustangs good image makers. With Shelby's extensive modifications these Mustangs, especially the GT 500 model, could outperform their competitors.

The pictures show Stephen R. Keusch's venomous Cobra G.T. 500. Functional air scoops abound and to help weight the hood is fiberglass. Seating was stock Mustang but the mahogany rim steering wheel and comprehensive instrumentation were unique to Shelby. A giant size 428 cu. in. V-8 provided the muscle. A colossal roll bar and hood pins accentuate the car's racing heritage.

Kaiser-Frazer wasn't doing too well by 1949 and a new small car was proposed by Henry J. Kaiser to help gee things up a bit. Shunning an attractive, small-car design from stylist Howard "Dutch" Darrin, Kaiser settled for a no-hoper concept from American Metal Products. 1951 was the Henry J's debut and it sold surprisingly well. After the initial spurt it was downhill all the way and production ended in 1954. Bill Arnold's mint Henry J. is a model powered by Kaiser's 161 cu. in. Supersonic six.

A radical design by Dutch Darrin was marketed by Kaiser as the Kaiser Darrin sportscar in 1954. Based on the Henry J's 100 in. wheelbase and powered by Willys' six cylinder, 90 hp engine, the K.D. was a unique concept. It was built from fiberglass and came with sliding doors and landau top. Tail lights were lifted from the Kaiser

Manhattan and the odd grille looked like a pair of pouting lips. The car was quite versatile with a top speed of 100 mph and thrifty, with 30 mpg.
Fred De Vault and William Clark own the car on these pages and it is one of only 435 built before Kaiser went under.

It started out as a Thunderbird but after Ford president, Robert McNamara saw the designs and said it should be the new Lincoln Continental, that is what it became. Launched in 1961, the new Continental was as different from its over-ornate predecessor as chalk is from cheese. It was also unique in many ways; being the only four door convertible model available anywhere, the doors opening from the center.

Tooling forward of the cowl was shared with Thunderbird to cut costs, though you couldn't tell.
The Continental's headlight bezels, joined by a chrome bar across the middle of the grille, are a styling feature almost identical to the '61 T-Bird. Dorothy and Jerry Coburn own this excellent example and use it for long distance travelling vacations.

Bowing to dealer insistance for a new Continental, Ford produced this Gordon Buehrig, John Reinhart, Bob Thomas design for 1956. It was unlike anything else on the market and assembly quality approached that of Rolls-Royce, as did the price. Each car cost $10,000 and even then Ford lost $1000 on each unit sold of this limited production automobile. Sales were disappointing and the Mk. II ended its run in 1957. Bob Edson of Hartford City, Ind., is the proud owner.

If ever there was a car that spoke for the fifties' youth then it has to be the 1949 – '51 Mercury. Its high waistline, rounded curves and narrow glass area begged customizing and its 255.4 cid L-head V-8 had enough guts for cruisin' down the boulevard on hot summer's nights. More often than not customizers dispensed with the sliced sausage grille for something much wilder and chopped the low roofline even lower. And the unusual fenderline was hard to resist.

The 1950 Mercury illustrated, belongs to Mike Butler of Auburn, who has known this car since his childhood. Previously owned by an old lady who knew of Mike's love for the car, it was passed on to him and remains his treasured possession.

Designed in America and built in England to American specifications, the Nash Metropolitan, brainchild of Nash president George Mason, went on sale in 1954. 83,442 cars later, the Metro ended its eight year run, a victim of Detroit's compact boom. Stylist Bill Flajole and engineer Meade Moore were the true creators of the Metropolitan. Austin of England was contracted to assemble the car using Austin's four cylinder A-40 engine, transmission and modified suspension parts. In 1956 the engine was enlarged from 70 to 90 cid. Because there was no trunk lid until 1959, the spare wheel was carried continental fashion at the rear. Vernon D. Crews owns this mint 1957 example.

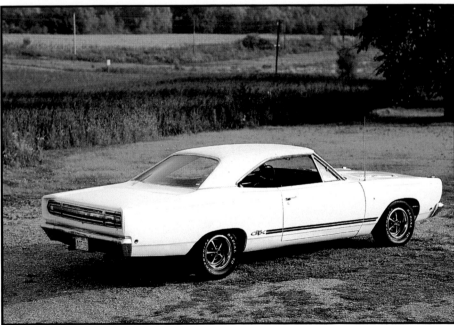

Imagine 0 – 60 in 6.3 seconds, the ¹/₄ mile in 14 at a speed of 96.5 mph, a top end speed of 130 plus and 9 – 15 mpg. That's what you would have expected from a Plymouth Belvedere GTX straight off the showroom floor in 1968. The GTX was one of a stable of ultra hot Chrysler musclecars, the meanest machines around, especially if equipped with the hemi. 426 cid and 425 hp in stock tune. Those were the days when gasoline was plentiful and the oil companies happy for it to pour, unabated, down the gullets of a nation's increasingly thirsty cars. The GTX at first glance, looks as mild mannered as Clark Kent . . . that is until you notice the stripe, hood scoops and special wheels.

The tires are fat, the engine the 440 wedge and the suspension as hard as nails. You have to know how to drive the GTX; it doesn't matter how macho you are the, GTX will spit you out along with the pips if you are unable to master that awesome power up front. Jim Ringenberg, owner of this quite friendly looking machine basking in the late summer sun, knows how to handle its ferocity when it's riled. His GTX has a very positive four speed manual 'box and he tells you that, set up properly, he has

done the quarter mile in 12 seconds. And down south, where he originally comes from, the moonshine boys used hot Chrysler products to lose the revenue men. The illicit liquor stills spawned real drivers which in turn, spawned NASCAR in a roundabout sort of way.
The GTX is a product of a golden era still close enough for us to remember. Basking in the tranquil setting of ripening corn, its friend the cat seems to smile . . . because she knows what the GTX knows that we don't . . .

All the hoopla that went with the Judge – no doubt inspired by the Plymouth Roadrunner – disguised its true place in the musclecar scheme. It entered the fray in 1969, rather late in the day, as it happened. Not that this mattered unduly; it had, after all, the GTO's wealth of experience behind it.

Never mind the dainty pink stripes, everything worked. The hood scoops, the hood mounted tach, all were functional. Under the hood throbbed 400 cubic inches of Ram-Air engine which knocked up 0 – 60 times in little over 6 seconds.

Up front was Pontiac's rubbery Endura covered bumper painted the same color as the body. Combined with white lettered tires and mag-style wheels the Judge looked the part it meant to play.

The car shown belongs to Don Andrews.

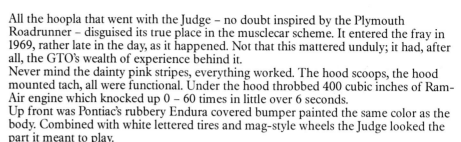

Arguably the most attractive of the three year cycle of two seater Thunderbirds was the 1957 model, shown here. Slightly longer than the 1955/56 models, the last two seat T-Bird had modest tailfins flanking the lengthened trunk area. A combined front bumper/grille treatment worked commendably well. Retained from 1956 was the optional bolt-on hardtop complete with glass "portholes" which was light enough for one man operation. This fine specimen is on show at the A-C-D Museum, Auburn, Ind.

Pictures *top and facing page* depict a husky 1967 Pontiac GTO. One of the fastest cars of the decade, the '67 GTO, with a 400 cu. in. V-8, 10.75:1 compression ratio and 4 speed manual transmission, could do zero to 60 in 4.9 seconds! With the three speed automatic the time was 5.2 secs. It also took only 13.09 secs. and 106.5 mph to do the quarter mile from standstill. That is moving in anybody's book! This GTO is minus its

GTO letters on the front left hand grille and belonged to Don Ayres Pontiac, Fort Wayne.
The other car is Philip Speer's '67 Pontiac Le Mans Sport Coupe. It is the family version of the GTO and projenitor of the musclecar in 1964. Pontiac's Wide Track chassis even gave the Le Mans decent handling, but not as good as the GTO.

Two Studebakers, three years apart, feature on these pages. The black car is the 1953 model designed by Robert E. Bourke, chief of Loewy's Design Studio. This is a Commander State Regal Hardtop and is powered by Studebaker's 259 cid V-8. Owner Alfred Hadley uses his car for show and daily transportation, hence modern road wheels. The gold and white model is the 1956 Golden Hawk, also designed by Loewy's studio. It was the same body as the '53 but heavily facelifted with the inclusion of a new hood, small, classic style grille and rudimentary fins. Under the hood sat the big 352 cu. in. Packard engine. The car is on display at the A-C-D Museum.

Pictures *left and top* are of the Tucker, possibly the world's most advanced automobile in 1948. Only 50 were made before Preston Tucker's dream ended in the courts. Styled by Alex Tremulis and Egan, the Tucker was very radical for its day. More importantly, it was mechanically very advanced. It had a full safety cockpit, pop out windshield in the event of an accident and a rear mounted aluminium flat opposed air cooled Franklin six displacing 335 cu. ins. The front center light turned with the wheels and the simple, but massive, grille/bumper arrangement conducted air into the car interior. If that wasn't enough, the doors cut into the roof and the Tucker had four wheel independent suspension. The Tucker was America's chance to get out in front

of everyone but she blew it! Pete Kesling owns this car which is on display at A-C-D museum.

Brook Stevens, the well known designer, was contracted by Willys to design a sporty family version of the company's wartime Jeep. Stevens' design was unusual and quite attractive and the Jeepster, as it was called, did reasonably well with first year sales of 10,000 plus. Both the 1948 and 1949 models had the traditional upright jeep grille but the center section was chromed and capped by a winged motive giving the appearance of an Indian totem pole. Paula Kash's 1949 Jeepster has a 63 hp four under its hood and Mrs. Kash did most of the restoration herself.

The first Lincoln Continental met public acclaim in 1940. It had a V-12 displacing 292 cu. in. and produced 120 hp at 3500 rpm. 1942 models were extensively restyled at the front end and the pointed hood of 1940 was replaced by a coffin nosed one. 1946 to 1948 Lincolns and Continentals picked up where they left off when interrupted by the war. About the only change was the grille pattern which was divided into vertical and horizontal bars. The L-head V-12 had five extra horsepower, otherwise it remained the same. This Continental courtesy the A-C-D Museum, Auburn, Ind.